CLEANSED

CLEANSED

A Catholic Guide to Freedom from Porn

By Marcel LeJeune

Pauline
BOOKS & MEDIA
Boston

Library of Congress Cataloging-in-Publication Data

LeJeune, Marcel.
   Cleansed : a Catholic guide to freedom from porn / by Marcel LeJeune.
      pages cm
   Includes bibliographical references.
   Summary: "A practical and spiritual guide to freedom and healing from pornography addiction from a Catholic perspective"-- Provided by publisher.
   ISBN 978-0-8198-1653-5 (pbk.) -- ISBN 0-8198-1653-1 (pbk.) 1. Pornography--Religious aspects--Catholic Church. I. Title.
   BV4597.6.L45 2016
   241'.667--dc23
                        2015029069

Excerpts from papal audiences, homilies, angelus messages, addresses, messages, and exhortations, copyright © Libreria Editrice Vaticana. All rights reserved.

The Scripture quotations contained herein are from the *New Revised Standard Version Bible: Catholic Edition,* copyright © 1989, 1993, Division of Christian Education of the National Council of the Churches of Christ in the United States of America. Used by permission. All rights reserved.

Excerpts from the English translation of the *Catechism of the Catholic Church* for use in the United States of America, copyright © 1994, United States Catholic Conference, Inc., Libreria Editrice Vaticana. Used with permission.

Cover design by Rosana Usselmann

Cover photo by istockphoto.com/ © AlexZaltsev

Published by Pauline Books & Media, 50 Saint Paul's Avenue, Boston, MA 02130-3491

Printed in the U.S.A.

www.pauline.org

Pauline Books & Media is the publishing house of the Daughters of St. Paul, an international congregation of women religious serving the Church with the communications media.

1 2 3 4 5 6 7 8 9   20 19 18 17 16

Contents

Foreword

Cleansed is a perfect title for this Catholic guide to freedom from porn. Marcel LeJeune does not sidestep the alarming and grotesque proportions of the current epidemic of pornography, nor does he hesitate to detail the devastating effects of the scourge of porn addiction on individuals, relationships, and society. The underlying theme he weaves throughout the book, however, is the good news that there is indeed a path to freedom from pornography use and addiction, and that the Catholic faith offers real hope to anyone struggling with porn. There are effective ways to be restored, healed, liberated, forgiven . . . cleansed.

Pornography has a long history. While some continue to debate what constitutes porn, the *Catechism of the Catholic Church* is very clear:

> *Pornography* consists in removing real or simulated sexual acts from the intimacy of the partners, in order to display them deliberately to third parties. It offends against chastity because it perverts the conjugal act, the intimate giving of spouses to each other. It does grave injury to the dignity of its participants (actors, vendors, the public), since each one

becomes an object of base pleasure and illicit profit for others. It immerses all who are involved in the illusion of a fantasy world. (no. 2354)

Our author puts it simply in these words: "Pornography is material that portrays suggestive behavior in order to arouse sexual desires and reactions."

The all too evident reality is that over-sexualized and pornographic imagery saturates our culture. It is available everywhere and to everyone. The Internet, for all of its benefits, has made pornography instantly accessible and seemingly anonymous. Everyone is vulnerable: men and women, young and old, married and single, laity as well as clergy and people in consecrated life. Pornography production and use is always harmful and always wrong. Yet there are ways to escape its grasp.

Marcel LeJeune writes convincingly about why porn matters and the damage it does to individuals, families, and society in his first two chapters. In Chapter 3, "How Did We Get into This Mess and How We Can Get Out?" he notes the currents of relativism, utilitarianism, and hedonism, which are so pervasive in our time and that are behind much of the sexual chaos that confronts us. He underscores the effect of the contraceptive mentality in stripping sex of its intended purpose—"babies and bonding"—with the result that pornography redefines the purpose of sex as pleasure alone. The world of porn disregards, denigrates, and denies the beautiful gift of human sexuality as God has designed it—for procreation and for the union of the spouses.

In the early chapters of the book, LeJeune offers a compelling analysis of the problem. His style of presentation engages not only those who are already struggling with pornography, but also others—parents, educators, clergy, counselors—who share the author's concern and commitment to help people become free of this burden.

The rest of the book, filled with realistic and promising advice and strategies, offers a well-reasoned and very practical action plan, a path to freedom from porn. At the center of the path to being cleansed is the Good News of Jesus Christ who, in the power of his mercy, restores hearts, heals wounds, forgives sin, and opens wide the door to new and abundant life. Christ can also transform our culture when we who are his missionary disciples agree to share in his work. This is a central dynamic of the New Evangelization.

Chapter 4, "Strategies for Individuals Who Struggle with Porn" details "18 Strategies to Stop"—from getting rid of all porn and future access to it, to finding an accountability partner and group, to regular exercise, as well as avoiding alcohol while engaging in the battle to overcome the temptation. Several of the strategies are specifically religious such as regular participation in the Eucharist and confession, prayer, fasting, and Scripture reading, Marian devotion, and involvement in service to others. The recommendation to seek professional help is the last strategy listed, but clearly an important one for anyone who is frustrated by unsuccessful efforts to win the battle against porn.

A highlight of this book is the chapter entitled "Virtue is NOT a Dirty Word." We need to do a far more effective job teaching our people (and that includes ourselves) about virtue. The theological virtues of faith, hope, and charity, given us by God in Baptism and strengthened in Confirmation, are at the heart of Christian discipleship. Then there are the human virtues, defined in the *Catechism of the Catholic Church* as "firm attitudes, stable dispositions, habitual perfections of intellect and will that govern our actions, order our passions, and guide our conduct according to reason and faith" (no. 1804). These virtues, like our bodies' muscles, must be exercised in order to grow strong. Like every Christian, the man or woman struggling with pornography will find the virtues of patience, chastity, humility, perseverance, and temperance to be potent medicine in the journey toward healing and forgiveness.

The book concludes with a look at the Catholic antidote to porn, an attitude that is rooted in our finding our identity as human persons in Jesus Christ and living fully in God's love, truth, and grace. The author calls upon Saint John Paul II's teaching on the theology of the body as a needed counterpoint to contemporary ideas about sex. It communicates a new path for us, one that is, our author assures us, "a path of freedom, holiness, and purity. It calls us to love and virtue. . . . [I]t rightly teaches us the holy purpose of our bodies."

I am grateful to Marcel LeJeune for this thoughtful, engaging, and very practical book. In the face of the challenge of pornography in our day, this book is a timely, much-needed, and promising resource in response to an urgent pastoral need.

Most Reverend Richard J. Malone, Th.D., STL
Bishop of Buffalo
Chairman, USCCB Committee on Laity, Marriage, Family, and Youth

Author's Note

If you are using porn and want to stop, there is hope!

This book contains direct and honest language about sexuality. It is not meant to be read by children. Nor is this book a substitute for professional help, if needed, by those who suffer from sexual addiction. Rather, this book offers hope and practical strategies for those who are caught up in pornography and for their families. It can also help families prevent pornography from entering their homes. Yet this book, by itself, won't cure any addict. The answer, instead, is to choose to accept God's love and grace into our hearts. Then we can live a life pleasing to God, even if that means taking the narrow path, humbling ourselves by seeking help, and changing the ways we act day to day.

I am a husband, a father, and a Catholic campus minister who has seen many lives crushed by pornography and other sexual wounds. Although I am not a counselor, a psychologist, or a priest, I have also seen lives transformed by forgiveness, grace, love, virtue, and sexual healing. In fact, what I love most about my job is being able to witness conversion of hearts and lives.

If you believe you are a sexual addict or someone who can't seem to find the inner strength to turn away from sexual brokenness and sin, I hope you will seek help. If you struggle with your sexuality, then do not hesitate to seek and find someone who can help you take the next step to sexual health and wholeness. It is worth whatever sacrifice you might need to make. While I don't claim that this book is the cure-all for sexual problems, I believe it can help many people turn their lives around.

Acknowledgments

Most books grow out of the stories, experiences, relationships, and conversations that each author learns about and experiences in life. This book is no different. Of course, I must first give all glory to Jesus Christ, who is the Way, the Truth, and the Life. If you haven't yet chosen to make Jesus your Lord, I pray that you will do so. No other path we can walk can bring us to everlasting happiness.

I can never thank my wife and children enough for the sacrifice they make when I write. When I write, I write at home, and I close the door. This means I take time from all of them and give it to a book; so I say to them: I thank you for being such an understanding and loving family. I love you all beyond words: Kristy, Kyra, Dominic, Olivia, Anna, and Elise.

I also thank all those who have contributed to this book in any way: friends and family who have encouraged me to write it; Bob Rice for his ideas; the many unnamed individuals who have allowed me to minister to them; those who have helped me in my own walk with Jesus; as well as those who have opened their lives to me, and who have helped me in my own walk with Christ.

Finally, I thank all the men and women who have shared with me their personal struggles. You have challenged me, humbled me, and taught me so much—thank you. I pray daily for all of you who struggle with your sexuality.

Introduction

You aren't perfect. I'm not perfect. None of us is. Yet the amazing thing about our imperfection, which we riddle with sin, is that despite it all God's love for us never stops. As a young adult I felt inadequate, unworthy, and humiliated because of my bad habits and sin. Yet I still chased after happiness by seeking sex and using others. It never worked. None of those things ever brought lasting happiness. They brought brief moments of pleasure, but those never lasted. I got through it all only because of an encounter with Jesus that shook me to the core. I finally found the love I had wanted all along!

All those who use pornography have a warped understanding of their self-image, their dignity, what it means to be a man, what it means to be a woman, relationships, family, love, God, guilt, forgiveness, and sex. This is why everyone—man, woman, or child—will struggle once they start using porn. It warps us. It attacks the very core of our humanity, and it will lay waste to our joy and peace.

It isn't enough to ignore the realities of what porn does to us and others or to simply try and justify our actions. To use porn is to accept a lie about love instead of continuing to look for the real thing. No regular user of pornography is able to see himself or herself (or any other human) in the way each person is meant to be seen: as a reflection of the Creator.

I have been working with sex addicts since I first entered campus ministry in 2002. I have seen many college students, children, parents, clergy, grandparents, and single people during this time. No part of our society is untouched by pornography. Soon after I began working in ministry, I realized that I was unequipped to deal with the problem. So I started doing some research, only to find that the Catholic Church had few resources at the time to help those struggling with their sexuality. Not giving up, I started reading about sexual addiction, the effects of pornography, and the mounting scientific and practical evidence that pornography damages individuals, families, and society. This convinced me that I had to do something and find help somewhere.

I eventually heard of a research facility that specialized in the study of addiction and found two professionals there who were doing studies in sexual addiction, recovery, and how to work with people of faith. It was a good fit for both parties. I needed their expertise in recovery and addiction, and they needed people of faith to work with. We started a collaboration that lasted for years.

Our collaboration helped me to learn about the science of how addiction affects the pleasure center of the brain and how it rewires the neural synapses that are meant to help us seek what is good for us. The researchers started to find, however, that most sex addicts who tried to stop on their own failed miserably. This meant that if I wanted to help those who were asking me for assistance, I would have to give them more than a good book or a presentation. They needed my love and my time.

I started to learn how faith could be used in helping others by modeling how to integrate prayer, spirituality, Scripture, and the theological virtues (i.e., faith, hope, and love) into the day-to-day struggles of the sex addict. I also learned some small group techniques of working with those who struggle with their sexuality. While I am not a professional counselor or therapist, I still use some of the best practices of those disciplines in the accountability groups I work with.

But no group is without struggles. I found out a lot about what to do and what not to do—often by doing the wrong thing. I also learned that God's grace is more than enough to conquer any issue, no matter how powerful it is. Furthermore, I learned something that every reader of this book should know: nothing you can do will make God stop loving you! Our actions are never powerful enough to stop God's love for each person, no matter what we have done. Our Lord's tenderness and mercy never end. We need only go to him humbly to receive the power of his love. True freedom from the unhappiness of porn cannot be found without God, because our sexuality (not just the other parts of our lives) needs redemption and grace to be properly ordered.

This is true freedom: living as we ought to live and living within the love of Jesus Christ, not merely doing whatever we want. True freedom is found in the person of Jesus Christ—who is Truth itself—which is why this book is ultimately about the interior battle each person wages. The goal of this book is to help you find freedom and healing in your own life and family and to shield your home from the evil of pornography, to protect yourself and those you love.

I want to reiterate: this book cannot substitute for professional help for a sex addict. If you believe you are sexually addicted, by all means follow the advice in the book, but don't stop there. Please seek professional help. Even if you are not an addict and have a history of struggling with your sexuality, a good professional counselor (a Catholic or Catholic-friendly one is highly preferable) can almost certainly help you. Don't let the fear of counseling, psychology, or the like stand in your way to a healthy, happy, and better life.

CHAPTER 1

Why Porn Matters

For you were bought with a price; therefore glorify God in your body. (1 Cor 6:20)

No child has ever wanted to grow up to be a sex addict. In fact, no adult in his right mind would ever want a sex addiction either. Yet we are quickly becoming a culture of sex addicts who casually hype our addictions as a healthy personal expression of our individuality. Nothing could be further from the truth. Consider Jimmy's story—a sex addict who never wanted the life he found himself in at the age of thirty-five, when he was already married and had children.

When Jimmy was three, his parents divorced. He bounced between his mom's house and his dad's house year after year. Neither of his parents seemed to want him around, and he certainly didn't connect with either of them. By the time Jimmy was ten, both of his parents had remarried and Jimmy had several step-brothers. He didn't get along with any members of his new family, and he never felt comfortable in his own skin. He disliked the way he looked, and that lead him to disliking who he was. By the time he was a teenager, he had learned to hide his self-loathing with a macho persona that portrayed confidence, but inside he hid fear, self-hatred, hurt, and insecurity.

Jimmy had seen magazines portraying nude women as a young boy, because his older step-brothers had them. He was fascinated by the bodies of the women he saw and thought about them frequently. He started to visit a certain neighbor's house a lot more because he knew he would have easy access to the stash of magazines kept in the garage. The boys would constantly tease one another about wanting to look at the magazines, but their curiosity would always be stronger than the desire to avoid a bit of pestering. Porn became a frequent habit, and masturbation wasn't far behind.

By the time Jimmy got to high school, he had gone through different phases of indulging his desire for porn and masturbation while also yearning to quit looking at it and to gain some self-control. But he found he couldn't stay away from it for more than a month or two at most. It was as if a Siren were always calling him back to her. He didn't have the strength to get away.

Once Jimmy got into college he found even more opportunities for sex all around him. Most of his buddies had porn in their dorm rooms; strip clubs would let him in once he could drink legally, and he even started to have "hook-ups" with women he met. After several years of sleeping with a number of young women, Jimmy fell in love with one of them. Deb was the girl of his dreams. She was willing to have sex with him, which seemed like the best of everything he had ever wanted. He was head over heels in love with Deb and felt he would do anything for her—anything but stop looking at porn and masturbating.

After several years of dating, they were married. Because they had frequent sex, Jimmy didn't look at porn quite as much, but he never gave it up completely. Then, after their first child was born, Deb and Jimmy couldn't have sex for an extended period. Jimmy went right back to porn. It didn't tell him to wait, like Deb did. It didn't need foreplay or have to feel "in the mood," like she did. In fact, porn never said no to Jimmy. It was the mistress always willing to appease him.

After a few years, Deb started to put on a few pounds, and Jimmy just wasn't as attracted to her as he once was. Deb started to notice a growing distance in their relationship. They rarely had sex and Jimmy wasn't interested in spending much time with her anymore. They started to argue more, and the tension between them was almost palpable. She felt as if he didn't love her anymore, and she started to resent Jimmy. In turn, Jimmy turned more and more to porn. During this time a younger coworker started to make passes at him.

The temptation seemed like a pornographic fantasy come to life, so Jimmy had an affair. Deb didn't find out until three years later, at which time she kicked him out of the house for a month. By that time they had two kids who couldn't understand why Daddy wasn't at home anymore.

Jimmy finally broke off his affair, and Deb convinced him to start counseling. They found that the root of their problems was a porn addiction that started when Jimmy was young. His self-loathing, his broken family, his failure to deal with his problems—all of these were papered over with a porn problem that masked his pain. Now thirty-five, Jimmy feels his life is going nowhere. As a couple, Jimmy and Deb desperately want to get out of the mess they have found themselves in, but the pain sometimes seems like too much.

This story of Jimmy and Deb is not the story of any one couple, but rather it describes the experiences of so many couples who struggle with porn addiction. I have devised it in order to highlight the core issue: porn destroys lives—not just the lives of the person who has the addiction, but those close to the person as well. Our society rarely talks about the reality of what happens to porn addicts and their relationships. Sex is powerful. It has the power to lead people to grow in love and to create life. But when it is misused, it also has the power to destroy.

The Power of Sex

Sex is the most powerful thing a man and woman can do together, because the sexual act makes new life. All of us have our beginning in the sexual act. Sex is a participation in the creative act of forming unique, unrepeatable human beings who are created by God for an eternal destiny and a beautiful purpose. But pornography doesn't care for this understanding of sex. Rather, it mocks the power of sex. Porn tosses this power aside, portraying it as a distraction from the alleged true power of sex, which is pleasure.

Pornography is material that portrays suggestive behavior in order to arouse sexual desires and reactions. It takes many forms and is found in every media format currently available: TV, Internet, photographs, movies, books, magazines, phones, and gaming stations, for example. A good way to determine if something is pornographic is to ask yourself: "Does it depict lewd sexual behavior intended to arouse sexual desire?" If the answer is yes, there is a good chance it is porn.

Porn is available to everyone and doesn't discriminate against anyone. In fact, porn use crosses all boundaries of age, sex, race, sexual preference, religious affiliation, and profession. It is used by clergy and laity, old and young, men and women, straight and same-sex attracted. In fact, no group is immune to the appeal of porn. It preys on our instincts and desires, and then twists them into something they aren't intended for: using other people.

Working with college students, I have found that most people who use porn started at an early age, in their home. *If* their parents discovered they were using porn, that discovery took months or years. Porn users will tell you they mainly access porn in private, and many feel a deep sense of shame when using it. Furthermore, the feeling of shame may keep them from seeking the help they need to stop. Some are exposed at such an early age that they may not even know the full extent of what they are doing, because porn can be attractive (and toxic) to the youngest of children and the oldest of adults.

Unfortunately our culture's response to porn could be described as a shrug of the shoulders at best, and encouragement as a healthy part of our sex lives at worst. Our community standard now considers it more of a punch line in a sitcom than a menace to the health of our communities. Some tell themselves that everybody accesses porn and it isn't a big deal. You can find porn in supermarkets. It is available at the touch of a button on your remote control. It is accessible through phones, computers, and gaming systems. Others think it is depraved, gross, or even evil, but they don't work to prevent its spread, since it isn't (or so they think) in their house or family. All of these attitudes have helped porn grow into the cultural power-house it is today.

First Exposure

I still remember the first time I saw an image of a naked woman. It was during the movie *Conan the Barbarian*, which my parents never would have allowed me to see if they had known about it. I can still remember the first nude scene as if it were yesterday. I was about ten years old when I saw the images, and as many of you who are reading this book can understand, that image is burned into my brain forever. There is no way to get rid of the image, even if I try to ignore it.

The power of porn is evident to many of us when we think of the sex scenes from movies we have seen, because the most memorable images are those that contain nudity and sex. This is because our brains were created to grasp these images and store them, since sex has the ability to engage us so powerfully. God created us this way to link two spouses through sex. It is a kind of marital glue that bonds spouses one to the other. When sex is misused it can be destructive, yet the "glue" still works to stick images into your brain. When I was ten I may not have fully grasped what I had seen and what the movie had done to me, and I certainly couldn't have told you what pornography was. But it affected me forever.

Take a moment to think of the ease of access the children of our world have to pornography today. Think also of the graphic nature of these videos and images. What kind of impact do you think porn will have on the next generation? What kind of impact will those children, once grown, have upon the world at large? What does pornography's rapid growth and power over our culture mean for our grandchildren and their children? It frightens me to think of the social, relational, familial, and cultural consequences.

Porn and the Church

When you think of the Church's teachings on sex, is your first thought *no*? Many Catholics and non-Catholics believe that the Catholic Church has only negative things to say about sex, such as its dangers outside of marriage. I have to admit that, for a good portion of my life, that was what I thought about Catholicism and sex. I believe it was due to the way I had been taught as a child. More than anything we kids were taught to fear sex because it can cause disease and lead to teenage pregnancy. Not only that, it is a mortal sin outside of marriage. But the wider culture was selling sex as the greatest thing ever to happen. It was about pleasure, happiness, and fun! That was a big reason why I stopped practicing my faith as a young adult and why many others do as well. My sex education was a mixture of fear, anxiety, fascination, lust, and guilt. I primarily learned about sex through my brother, my friends, and pornography. It certainly didn't set me up for success. Rather, it turned into a recipe for disaster.

This is why porn, masturbation, and sex outside of marriage are still so powerful in our culture. Most people, both young and old, don't have a good enough reason to say no to porn, because the yes is so powerfully attractive. In fact, the Church's teachings seem boring if all they have to say is no.

Yet today the Church's teachings on sex are much more about its beauty and power. When we understand why a *no* once in a while can be good for each of us, it can help us realize that *yes* is much bigger and better. Nevertheless, this will only happen when we truly understand what God wants us to know about sex and why the Church teaches what it does, and then choose to make these teachings our own. We will dive more deeply into the Church's teachings later in this book, but for now you should know that the truth the Church teaches about sex is anything but boring.

We should not deny that the Church says no to the culture's failed idea of sexuality. The Church teaches that any sexual act between one man and one woman outside of a marriage is wrong. We could add many other things to the list of what ails our culture. They include divorce and remarriage, pornography, masturbation, sterilization, same-sex marriage, contraception, abortion, in-vitro fertilization, and so forth. All these activities harm us as individuals, as families, and as communities. They harm our entire culture. Just as any loving mother does, the Church points out to us those things that may harm us spiritually, mentally, emotionally, relationally, culturally, and even physically. If a toddler stretches a hand toward a boiling pot of water and the parent does not correct the behavior, then the parent does not choose to love the child in that moment. The same could be said of a church that teaches that improper sexual behavior is harmful yet keeps silent. So the Church teaches that any kind of sexual act or thought that isn't in accord with God's design may damage us.

The Church tells us this to guide and help us. This is a loving thing to do. In fact, to fail to do so would be an unloving act.

What Is True Love?

To properly understand our sexuality, we must start with a true understanding of love. My definition of love has developed over many years of reflection and teaching others about relationships. Love is *choosing what is best for the other person despite what it might cost the one who loves.* Love is not merely an emotion, a feeling, or an act of having sex with someone. Love is not something that comes and goes and we can't control; rather, it is a choice lived out in our daily lives. Love is not about what I as an individual get out of it.

Every time we choose to say no to one thing, we choose to say yes to something else. When a wife says no to an extramarital affair, she says yes to her marriage, husband, and family. This also works in reverse, because every yes is a no to something else. When a father says yes to spending time with his kids, he says no to spending time doing something else. Therefore, saying no to porn is also saying yes to love and sexuality as they are meant to be lived out. Furthermore, any person who would say yes to loving others would say no to porn.

The moral teachings of the Church provide boundaries to guide our choices and help us have a proper understanding of what is good, true, and beautiful as we develop the internal habits and virtues that allow us to easily choose what is best for others and ourselves. These boundaries are not impositions on us, because we are still free to choose otherwise, even to the point of committing sin.

Yet if all we do is choose to follow the law, then no true conversion is taking place. In Romans 13:8, Saint Paul says, "The one who loves another has fulfilled the law." If I truly love my wife, I do not need to worry about breaking the sixth commandment on adultery. True love fulfills all that the law requires and goes beyond it. In the same way, if you truly love God, you would never even want to worship another god. The law is there to guide us and help us. But one who truly loves doesn't need the law anymore.

Too often the laws surrounding how Catholics ought to act have been the heart of what the Church has taught about sexuality. While we should not avoid the prohibitions of the laws, they should not be the focus of how we respond to the problem of pornography. No amount of fear tactics or negativity can sway someone away from porn once that person has been using it for a while. Rather than peddling what is bad, we need to focus on the beautiful and positive message that Christ has given us about sex. Sex can be a beautiful and amazing act, if we choose to use it in the manner God intended.

To help those who struggle with pornography, we will start with some recommendations and strategies that may be hard to follow. They might seem like an imposition, one that could even stifle our freedom and happiness. But the idea that unrestrained sex brings freedom and happiness is a lie. Our suggestions may seem difficult, because most virtues take hard work and time to develop. Most men and women will need discipline, accountability, support, prayer, and fortitude to make the changes necessary. The strategies are a first step, but not the final one. The ultimate goal is to develop virtue.

Virtue is the habit of doing what is good and true easily and quickly. But developing virtue doesn't come easily. Anyone who has tried but failed to stop using porn and/or masturbating knows this. Ultimately, porn has never brought anyone happiness—but virtue has. It is worth the time and effort.

Nobody ever wins a marathon without training. Neither will you win the battle over porn without training hard and changing your life. Building a life of virtue can lead to lasting and true happiness, which is what we are really seeking.

After examining this issue, some might want to know why others would ever use pornography if the results can be so devastating. The reason is simple: they believe it will make them happy, at least for a moment. Whenever we sin in any way, we are really looking to fulfill a desire for happiness. Sin might bring a moment's pleasure, but it never lasts. Porn might seem to help a person escape problems for a while, but it will create even more problems, and it never resolves the original ones.

I have found that the vast majority of those who struggle with porn have a lot of difficulty with relationships. Porn offers an imaginary relationship with an attractive person (or persons) who will never say no, who is always available and willing to have sex, and who won't hurt the seeker or need an emotional attachment. Of course, porn also results in despair, loneliness, and similar issues, because porn can't deliver on the promises it makes. Porn never brings love, peace, or lasting happiness.

Talking about a Revolution

The fruit of the sexual revolution is not only ripe, it is also rotten. We see it all around us in the daily headlines: teenagers who sext (send sexual pictures via text messaging) one another, same-sex marriage, the hook-up culture on college campuses,

free contraception as a "right" enshrined into government poli-
cies, human trafficking to support sex slavery, and the rise of
porn as a social norm. All of these issues, and others, have at
their core the false philosophy that sex is about pleasure alone.
This view sees the other issues normally attached to sex (such as
children, bonding of spouses, chastity) as merely tangential and
always optional.

Let us be honest, the Church has been slow and inadequate
in fashioning an effective response to the rapidly changing culture around us. In many ways Catholics have swept the issues
surrounding sexuality under the rug for so long that many are
either ignorant about just how bad it is or believe the Church's
teachings on sexuality are "out of date." Some Catholics don't
want to talk about sex because they are afraid they will be labeled
hypocrites in the light of recent sex abuse scandals. Still others
have a partial understanding of the Church's teachings and reject
them. Finally, some don't want to talk about these issues for fear
of being immodest or hurting a child's innocence.

We must have a better answer! We must propose a positive
alternative of love, life, health, relationships, marriage, family,
faith, and God. This means we must fight against pornography,
which degrades all of these good things. Porn tricks us into
believing other humans are not human at all, but rather objects
for our own selfish use. In our mind's eye we treat those involved
in porn as objects for our pleasure, not as other humans for
whom we truly want what is best.

Ultimately, porn leads us to the opposite of love. It is using
the highest of all of creation (other human beings) as objects. It
degrades and uses others as things. No human being—even
porn stars, prostitutes, and adulterers—was created to merely
be an object of lust!

Sex, like most things, can be used for good or evil. When sex is pornographic, it is always evil. Porn separates love from sex and raises pleasure as the sole goal. Once sex is no longer about love but about pleasure first, by definition it is selfish. You can't look at porn for your own pleasure and be doing it for the sake of others. In and of itself, it is an exercise of the ego—it is all about *me* and what I get out of it. Ultimately it degrades and punishes the very people the purveyors of porn claim to empower.

Don't be fooled into believing that porn is just a private issue. It is an exploitation of others in every way possible. It is a social problem because it affects marriages, families, relationships, children, groups, advertising, social norms, and other things. It is a spiritual problem not only for Catholics but also for Orthodox Christians, Protestants, Muslims, and Jews, who all believe it is sinful and harmful to our relationship with God. It is a mental problem because it can be highly addictive, and it is a physical problem because it changes our brains to function in a way they are not intended to.[1] We will explore these problems in depth in later chapters of this book.

Porn is ripping out the heart of millions of people and changing our world in a social experiment the likes of which we have never seen before. A pornographic mentality is at the heart of many of the problems in our culture today.

It is too late to stop the slide into a culture of pornography, because we are already there. What we can and must do now is

---

1. For more on the science of the brain, see *Wired for Intimacy: How Pornography Hijacks the Male Brain* as noted in the resources section of this book. —*Ed.*

reach into this culture and help one person at a time, by offering a life-giving alternative of freedom from the slavery that porn offers.

But freedom never comes without cost.

Activities and Questions

1. Why is sex so powerful? Do you think the power of sex can be misused? If so, what are some ways we can misuse sex? If you don't believe it can be misused, why not?

2. Do you remember your first exposure to pornography? What kind of thoughts and feelings did you have? Why?

3. How were you taught about sex? Was it a positive or negative experience? How did this affect you as you have gotten older?

4. Are you more likely to say no to porn or yes to something positive? Why?

5. Write down all the positive things about sex you can think of. Which one is the best reason to say no to porn and yes to something else?

Chapter 2

What Porn Does to Individuals, Families, and Society

Do not follow your base desires, but restrain your appetites.
(Sir 18:30)

NOTE—*the hypothetical scenario below makes a point by using a graphic image. I believe it can help others, especially parents, understand the magnitude of pornography.*

Imagine you are preparing dinner for your family and you hear a knock on the front door. You answer it to find a young man and a young woman who ask to see your child. Even though you don't know them, you allow them into your home. They make their way into your child's room, where they undress and have sex on your child's bed, while your child watches and becomes aroused. Of course, you would never let this happen in your home—no decent parent would. Yet millions of parents allow similar images to come into the hands of their children by allowing unfiltered Internet, TV, game systems, and phone use in their homes. It is merely a matter of time before a child either stumbles onto pornography or looks for it intentionally.

Even in good Christian families children can be exposed to pornography and develop an addiction. Children can be exposed while doing homework research online, or a friend or relative could show them porn. Still other children may hear about it and in innocent curiosity look for it on their own. Regardless of where the first exposure takes place, any child-hood exposure to porn is reprehensible.

As I have already said, pornography does not discriminate, even against children. Porn purveyors know that the younger they can hook a child on their materials, the more likely they are to gain a lifetime consumer. This is why they use many techniques to intentionally target youth.

Imagine the lifelong damage a child may suffer as a result of being sexualized by pornography at a young age. Porn teaches children a number of things, none of them good or healthy for an adult, much less a youth. The results are devastating not only to children who view porn but also to their families.

Beware!

Pornographers target those who have never seen porn in order to get more viewers and make more money. Pornographers know that families with children are the best place to get new consumers. No child is ever born with an addiction to porn. It is a learned behavior for every addict.

One common technique used to target new consumers involves purchasing Web site names that are either very similar to or intentional misspellings of legitimate Web sites. When a small portion of the millions who visit a high-traffic Web site stumble upon the misspelling, they are routed to a pornographic Web site. Many Web sites for children have been targeted by this technique.

Another technique pornographers use is to buy the name of a legitimate Web site when an owner allows the rights to that domain name to expire, often by accident or oversight. That site is then linked to pornography. The victim company must either take legal action or pay a premium to get the Web site name back.

Many other techniques are used. Sometimes pornographers automatically download spyware, Trojan horses, or viruses onto a computer after a user clicks on a Web site or e-mail link, allowing popup pornography to appear on their computer. In some cases, spam containing graphic images or links to pornographic Web sites is e-mailed. Another technique uses peer-to-peer and file-sharing apps to bypass browsers and content filters.

In finding new ways to target both adults and children, pornographers are industry leaders. They do not have a problem using immoral and sometimes even illegal practices to capture your attention. They have billions of dollars to use for this. With this kind of threat lurking around every virtual corner, we need to be vigilant in finding ways of helping our families safely navigate the Web, protecting them from those who wish to harm them.

Many parents might react to such threats by shutting down all technology in their house. While children are young, this is certainly an option. Yet I have found that teens and young adults need to be taught how to safely use the Internet and all the gifts it brings into our lives. They certainly won't be able to handle themselves all alone once they leave your house if you don't teach them how while they are in it. This training is best done in the safety of their own homes by parents who are diligent and knowledgeable about how they can help steer their children through these minefields. In a later chapter this book will offer many practical suggestions on how to do this.

Individuals

Pornography has a stronghold over many people. Part of its strength comes from the anonymous nature of the Internet, where most people now view it. Pride is a big factor in keeping such problems secret. If others don't know you have a problem, it can be humiliating to admit it to another person. We think others will believe we are not good people or that we are terrible sinners. But the truth is that addicts need the help of others to stop using pornography. While admitting our failures is humbling, it need not be humiliating.

If you don't know anyone to talk to, I recommend you seek out a good counselor, priest, or even a trusted friend. Your secret needs to be brought into the light. Admitting it to another person may be tough, but it can also be freeing, because you no longer have to carry the burden alone.

Many other issues are compounded when our sexuality is out of place. If one or both persons in a relationship is dealing with a pornography problem (or other serious sexual issue), it will have a profound and deep impact on the relationship itself.

There is no way to avoid it. This means other issues may arise—communication problems, feelings of being emotionally distant, co-occurring addictions or disorders, mental health problems, abuse, or others.

When you go to see someone about a porn problem, don't be shy about admitting the situation. Get it on the table as soon as you can. Most likely, the other person has heard of such a thing before. Of course, it takes courage to admit this problem, but most people will recognize that. I sometimes think more of someone for being able to admit a problem to me!

Many people are unsure of themselves because they don't know who they are. As we will explore deeply in chapter 10, this is the root of the problem. Pornography robs us of the eyes we need to see our own worth and the worth of others. Without the ability to see the truth about ourselves and the rest of humanity, we are unable to see the lies about pornography and other sexual sins.

If I meet someone whom I feel doesn't know his or her own identity, I ask that person if I can share something. If he or she agrees, I tell them that before the earth was made, our Father in heaven knew each of us. He knows you! He has had all of our names sealed upon his heart, and he thought about you when he made the world for us. Think about how beautiful are the sky, the oceans, the animals, and the plants. God has made all of them. Think about the grandeur of the mountains and the stars in the sky. Now think about this fact: they are nothing in comparison to you! When you were made, you were made in God's image and likeness; you were made with the ability to love, and no other earthly creature can love like we can! When God looks at you, he sees his son or daughter. He sees the greatest and most beautiful thing he has ever made! In fact, God loves you so much that he sent his only-begotten Son, Jesus, to earth to live, preach, heal, suffer, die, and rise again—for you. God did this in order to conquer sin and death, so that you could live in heaven with him forever!

This is how our God loves each of us. This is how God loves you. You were made with an eternal destiny and with a worth beyond measure.

Yet a person who hears this explanation may not know how to react. You might not, either. I recommend that you ask God to reveal to you the truth about your profound dignity. Ask him to help you and lead you to a deeper understanding of the reality of your nature. I know that you desire a love such as I have described, because we humans were made for it.

The confidence each of us needs to follow Jesus and to shed our sin is found only in grace—the free gift of God's love, which we can do nothing to earn. At some point we all need to understand God's love better and take hold of a personal faith in order to truly know what this love is like. We can only do this once we are free from the lies hidden under the surface of a culture of sex. Porn magnifies those cultural lies for us. Because of those lies, people who use porn are not free enough to see the truth about themselves, the other person, or their relationships.

Porn ruins lives.

Jesus restores them.

The Heart of the Matter

In working with young people who use porn, I have found they have one universally shared feeling after they discover their deep need and ask for help: shame. Shame is generally considered more than just regret or guilt. It is the humiliating feeling of unworthiness that accompanies those emotions. Shame builds on negativity about the very nature of the person, not just his or her actions.

Furthermore, those who experience shame have a deep feeling of uncertainty about themselves, including a lack of confidence. The feelings that many sex addicts and porn users have can spill over into their relationships, causing problems for others as well.

We know that men who look at pornography regularly have a much higher tolerance for sexually aggressive acts, aberrant sexual behaviors, promiscuity, and even rape.

Children who regularly look at pornography are at a real disadvantage. They are not mature enough to completely understand what they have seen, and this can stunt their sexual maturation. The harm is increased dramatically when they are exposed at a young age, and also after multiple experiences. These problems also occur when young people are morally insecure and uncertain in their beliefs about sex.[1]

The adolescent porn culture grows even worse when they become young adults. The frequency of porn use among males has been shown to dramatically increase their likelihood of having sex with nonromantic friends. Porn also likely contributes to the hook-up culture found on college campuses and within

---

1. Jochen Peter and Patti M. Valkenburg, "Adolescents' Exposure to Sexually Explicit Internet Material, Sexual Uncertainty, and Attitudes Toward Uncommitted Sexual Exploration: Is There a Link?" *Communication Research* 35 (2008): 579–601 (581).

the young adult culture (sex with an acquaintance, in the absence of any other kind of relationship).[2]

Once marriage and children enter the lives of those who use porn, the problems magnify as well. After long periods of looking at pornography, men have reported that they loved their wives less.[3] In fact, pornography use can be so devastating to a relationship that it has been shown to be as bad as having an affair, even though the object is a person on a screen.[4]

One study about cybersex ("sexual" interaction between at least two people via the Internet) revealed that more than half of those who engaged in it had lost interest in real-life sex with their partners. The partners, too, were affected deeply, with one third of them losing interest in sex. When put together, the results show that just one-third of couples with at least one partner using cybersex had sustained interest in sex in their real-life relationship![5]

Ultimately, repeated and prolonged exposure to pornography by spouses results in the death of a marriage. Too many

---

2. E. Häggström-Nordin, U. Hanson, and T. Tydén, "Associations between Pornography Consumption and Sexual Practices among Adolescents in Sweden," *International Journal of STD & AIDS* 16 (2005): 102–7 (104–5).

3. Dolf Zillmann and Jennings Bryant, "Pornography's Impact on Sexual Satisfaction," *Journal of Applied Social Psychology* 18 (1988): 438–53 (439–440), quoting S. E. Gutierres, D. T. Kenrick, and L. Goldberg (1983, August), *Adverse Effect of Popular Erotica on Judgments of One's Mate*, paper presented at the annual meeting of the American Psychological Association.

4. Jennifer P. Schneider, "Effects of Cybersex Problems on the Spouse and Family," *Sex and the Internet: A Guidebook for Clinicians*, ed. A. Cooper (New York: Brunner-Routledge, 2002): 169–86 (180).

5. Jennifer P. Schneider, "Effects of Cybersex Addiction on the Family: Results of a Survey," *Sexual Addiction & Compulsivity* 7 (2000): 39–40.

divorces have happened because one or both spouses used porn. With the growing acceptance of pornography as a social norm, the divorce rate will undoubtedly rise.

Other statistics prove that pornography is more widespread than people imagine, and it is also ruining relationships, destroying lives, and hurting us all. Sexual permissiveness, openness to nontraditional relationships, an acceptance of immoral practices, and even a higher tendency toward violence all result from pornography.

The science is overwhelming, yet our culture is slow to respond. This is because we have been lulled into a belief that pornography is mostly benign. It is not. Rather, it is a cancer that is starting to metastasize within our culture. No culture has ever survived such sexual permissiveness and neither will our own, unless it changes radically and quickly.

Activities and Questions

1. What part of this chapter did you find most surprising or shocking? Why?

2. Do you believe our culture has a healthy or unhealthy view of sexuality? If you believe it is healthy, in what ways and why is it healthy? If you believe it is unhealthy, in what ways and why is it unhealthy?

3. Do you believe God loves you even when you do something bad? Do you believe you are lovable? Why or why not?

4. Read the story of the Prodigal Son in Luke 15:11–32. Now read it again, but imagine yourself as the prodigal son. How does it feel to go home to your father? What is

it like to experience love and forgiveness when you don't believe you deserve it? Do you believe God loves you the same way? Why or why not?

CHAPTER 3

How Did We Get into This Mess and How Can We Get Out?

Create in me a clean heart, O God. (Ps 51:10)

In my childhood, pornography was certainly not a public or typical part of our culture. In fact, it was taboo. No civic, political, or religious leader wanted anything to do with it. Still, it was in the background, seeping into our lives in unspoken ways: the magazines a father of a friend kept in his house; the "adult" cable channels most people didn't subscribe to, but some hotels did; the videos being shown late at night in a college dorm. While the wider culture rarely talked about it, porn was slowly working its way into our world. But where did it all start? To understand that we have to understand recent history.

Contraception and Sexual Chaos

Contraception is at the root of many cultural issues, especially the fundamental reorienting of how most people understand the purpose of sex. But before we can see how a contraceptive mentality has gotten us into such a sexual mess, we have to understand the ideas behind the wide acceptance of sexual chaos.

The underlying philosophies of our modern culture are relativism, utilitarianism, and hedonism. Relativism is the philosophy that truth, especially moral truth, is relative to persons, places, times, cultures, or situations. In this school of philosophy, there are no universal moral norms that apply to all people, places, times, and situations. Relativism says that truth is subjective, changing according to the circumstances. Therefore, no truth is universal or binds us to universally objective truth, which is above us. Of course, this philosophy is self-defeating. If there is no absolute truth, how can you absolutely know that? Believing there is no absolute truth is itself an absolute truth. Furthermore, moral relativists are usually morally relative in practice only. When they feel morally violated, they believe in rules that bind others.

Without objective moral absolutes, no sin or human failure can be deemed evil. No action can be wrong at all times. This leads to a morally lax society in which everyone can do whatever he or she pleases, regardless of consequences. Relativism is a philosophy that will ultimately be the end of any society that owns it.

Utilitarianism—the philosophy that the point of life is to maximize benefits and minimize negatives, especially suffering —flows naturally from relativism. According to this way of thinking, the ends justify the means. But a problem arises with this philosophy because sometimes the means *are* evil. For example, when having another baby would cause difficulties for a woman, the "good" of not having to care for another child (the end) means an abortion (the means) can be a "good" thing. In a moral universe, the "good" of not having a baby does not justify killing a child to achieve that goal. We must have both a good end and means in order for any act to be morally good.

Hedonism is the little brother of utilitarianism. Building on the idea of maximizing happiness and minimizing suffering, hedonism promotes pleasure-seeking primarily by using other people and things to attain a person's happiness, especially sex-ually. Hedonism allows humans to use other people as objects, often as sexual objects. Again, the ends justify the means.

These are the corrosive philosophies of modern times, when contraception is so widely accepted and allowed. This contra-ceptive mentality has changed us as a people. Sex is merely for pleasure, however we can get it and as we wish it to be. Sex is not for making babies or for bringing two spouses together. It is purely a selfish act of fulfilling a "need," not a giving of self to another.

This contraceptive mentality is especially easy to see in how many of us think about children: Parents have a "right" to chil-dren and can create them in petri dishes, if needed. They can also dispose of them through abortion if they want to. Having power over our sexuality and doing with it whatever we please is now a given in a culture that has widely accepted contracep-tion not only as the norm, but also as a good thing.

Contraception makes people turn inward, rather than out-ward—it perpetuates selfishness on their part and that of their sexual partners. It also makes people see marriage as an optional social construct (an attitude that harms women and children most). This mentality is tearing our culture apart. It happens when sex between two people becomes about "me" rather than "you." The fruits of our modern culture include abortion, divorce, fatherless homes, porn, and other ills, none of which helps us as a people. Rather, they reflect a culture obsessed with individual autonomy and the license to do whatever the individual pleases.

When sex isn't about babies or the bonding of spouses, it becomes selfish. Once sex becomes a selfish activity, the family breaks down. Everyone knows that selfishness in families brings misery and a failure to bond. Yet independence and the freedom to do as we please are vaunted above all things, including the family. Once the family breaks down, society breaks down. How did we get to this point?

1930

All of Christianity rejected contraception until 1930, when the Lambeth Convention of the Anglican Church allowed it in narrow circumstances. Just a few years later, a Protestant group of denominations (the Federal Council of Churches, now the National Council of Churches) accepted it. Though most Christians at the time still opposed contraception, that attitude changed after only a few decades.

At the time, our society had a commonsense attitude toward contraception. This cultural rejection of contraception wasn't something new; even the Protestant reformers unanimously rejected contraception. Contraception was against the law in the United States until 1965. In that year the Supreme Court ruled in *Griswold v. Connecticut* that it was legal for married people to use birth control. In Canada contraception was legalized in 1969, along with abortion.

Our choices in light of this history are

1. Either nearly two thousand years of consistent Christian tradition (and the current stance of the Catholic Church) is wrong, or

2. All of Christianity had it wrong (and the Catholic Church still does) until the twentieth century. The truth was uncovered in the midst of a sexual revolution during the most violent century the world has ever known.

Of course, many "saw" what the future would hold if contraception was legal and widely used: marriages would be better, unwanted pregnancies would decrease, and abortions would decrease. But what has happened? The divorce rate has gone up significantly. Broken families are now the norm. Pregnancy is only valued when a baby is "wanted." Abortion is used as a backup when contraception fails.

Paul VI

In his groundbreaking 1968 encyclical *Humanae Vitae*, Pope Paul VI predicted the following would happen if contraception was widely used:

1. "How wide and easy a road would thus be opened up toward conjugal infidelity and the general lowering of morality." Think about the increase in affairs. We now

make them a public display on daytime talk shows, with lie detector tests and dramatic arguments. Watching a family being torn apart is considered entertainment!"

2. "It is also to be feared that the man, growing used to the employment of anticonceptive practices, may finally lose respect for the woman and, no longer caring for her physical and psychological equilibrium, may come to the point of considering her as a mere instrument of selfish enjoyment, and no longer as his respected and beloved companion." Of course, porn and an increase in rape, selfishness, hooking up, and so forth have all proved this prediction true.

3. "Who will stop rulers from favoring, from even imposing upon their peoples, if they were to consider it necessary, the method of contraception which they judge to be most efficacious? In such a way men, wishing to avoid individual, family, or social difficulties encountered in the observance of the divine law, would reach the point of placing at the mercy of the intervention of public authorities the most personal and most reserved sector of conjugal intimacy." This was fulfilled first in China with its one-child policy, which led to forced abortions when the policy was broken. Yet even in the United States the federal government has been forcing Catholics to purchase contraception for others, despite their conscientious objection, with the Health and Human Services contraceptive mandate.

Pope Paul VI, among others, was able to predict what would happen because he knew the frailty of human nature, with its tendency to seek sin. He also knew that wide cultural acceptance of immoral practices helps others to rationalize sinful behavior. Using a Christian understanding of nature, the human person, and sin, he rightly predicted the pornographic culture we live in today.

Paul VI also understood that when human beings use other human beings as objects, bad things happen. If I want to set up a successful business, I ought not to deceive or cheat my customers. In the same way, if we want to behave according to our purpose, we'd better not use our sexuality in a sinful manner.

Purpose of Sex

Most people seem to assume that sex is merely for pleasure. But God didn't create us just to have a good time in bed. Sex has two purposes: the first purpose is babies (for spouses to procreate), and the second purpose is the union of the two spouses (bonding between persons, which helps seal the relationship).

If we take either purpose out, then sex loses its meaning and becomes something it was never intended to be. For example:

> ⊳ Premarital sex: sex without commitment certainly can't bond people together.

> ⊳ Rape: sex without consent is neither for babies or bonding.

Because God intends for sex to be an act of love, it plays a part in the relationship between husband and wife. When sexual union occurs outside this bond of love (marriage), then it is no longer a purely loving act. Remember how we define love— choosing what is best for others, despite the cost to ourselves. With this in mind, premarital sex is never an act of love. To willfully take a risk with someone's well-being is not love, and premarital sex risks another person's health—emotionally, spiritually, relationally, and physically (for instance, break-ups, sin, or disease). Furthermore, when possible, children should have both a stable family with one father and one mother.

When sex loses its intended purpose, it becomes something that isn't about love or the other person. It becomes selfish. But sex is made to be wonderful, loving, and awe-inspiring. In fact, as Catholics we say sex is even better than good—we say it has a holy and Godly purpose.

Theological/Biblical Reasons

From the way the modern world talks about children and portrays them in the media, what dominant view of them emerges? Clearly, many people believe that having children will impinge on a couple's money, freedom, and happiness, and even drain the earth's resources. In other words, children are an unnecessary burden.

But the Bible has a different view of children. In fact, every instance of infertility in the Bible is considered a curse. Similarly, every fertile couple is considered blessed. Thus, God sees children as blessings that he bestows on his people. Children are gifts from God. In fact, the earth is made for us, not vice versa.

As persons destined for eternal life, we can participate with God in creating new life. When we create with God (procreate), we add to his glory and allow more infinitely valuable people to have the opportunity to be with him forever in heaven.

God designed married sex to be open to life. When a couple has sex and uses contraception, they are, in effect, telling God that they want to have the secondary part of sex (pleasure) without its primary purpose. It is as if a couple says to God— "no thanks God, we don't really want you to be present to us in this part of our lives."

So contraception achieves three things. First, it attempts to block God out of the creative part of the sexual act. Second, it treats children more as a burden or curse than a blessing or gift from God. Third, it prevents the spouses from fully giving every part of themselves to one another and blocks their full bonding. These three effects help us to realize how contraceptive sex cannot achieve the Godly purpose of sex. If love is a total self-giving of oneself to another, then to withhold fertility from a spouse is to give a partial gift at best. At worst, it is using the spouse as an object, which is the opposite of love.

To sum up the results of contraceptive sex, think about which of the following phrases best describes love between two spouses—"I want to have sex with you" or "I love you. I want to spend the rest of my life with you and have children with you." One is about me. One is about the other person.

Porn is always about me and never about others. Love is always about the other person.

From Contraception to Porn

The attitudes about sex that are born from a contraceptive mentality lead directly to an openness to pornography. If sex is about pleasure for me, then it has nothing to do with other people, unless they can bring me pleasure. Porn is a natural result of such an attitude. So are infidelity, the hook-up culture, sleeping around, the wide acceptance of same-sex marriage, and similar ills.

Our culture has accepted the porn epidemic without any kind of critical assessment. Notice how debates about porn are framed more about individual "rights" to do as one wishes rather than how destructive porn can be.

To sum it up, contraception strips sex of its intended purpose (i.e., babies and bonding), and pornography completely redefines sex as pleasure alone. Therefore, we are now at a point in our hedonistic world where we can't even agree about the purpose of sexuality. People object: Who are you to say that what someone else does is wrong? Who are you to say that others shouldn't have sexual pleasure in whatever way they want?

We have given away much and the stakes are high. So what do we do?

The Good News

The good news is that we have the Good News—the Gospel of Jesus Christ. Christ can restore hearts. Christ can forgive sin. Christ can change our culture, but only when we agree to do his work on earth. So we have to do our part. This is the action plan.

First, we have to pray for our culture and for all people. We can't accept only those who agree with us. If we go that route, how can we change anything? No, we need to love those who do not love us. We need to serve those who don't like us. We need to talk to those who disagree with us. We can only do this when we truly love all the other humans God puts in our lives. Thus, we can't see anyone as the "enemy."

We have to educate ourselves first and then others. Do we truly know what the Church teaches about sexuality? Can we explain it in a positive way that can attract those who don't want to hear what we have to say? If not, we have to educate ourselves and help other Christians (and non-Christian allies) see what the truth is.

We have to vote according to our morals and faith. We have to engage our public representatives and institutions to see porn as a danger to our society and help build up safeguards for those vulnerable to porn, especially children.

We have to speak up and let others know we don't like what is happening to us, our children, and our world. We have to do what might be uncomfortable for many of us, that is, speak directly to a culture that may reject what we have to say.

We also have to turn off media that promotes porn. Those outlets thrive because not only are Christians silent in allowing it, but many also support it and buy it. Money is the driving force behind it all. Pornographers merely provide a product to those who want it.

Ultimately, this is a battle for hearts, which means we have to evangelize others so God can change their hearts. We cannot make someone choose anything, nor would we ever want to force them to do so anyway. Rather, we want to help them find what is really beautiful, true, and good in our world. This battle for our culture is not lost yet.

Changing Culture

Here are eleven ways Christians can transform our modern culture.

1. **Work on ourselves first.** We can fully control only our own decisions. If we want to influence our culture or make any positive change, then we need to work on our

own lives. The only way to do this is to abandon ourselves to God's grace.

2. **Evangelize, evangelize, evangelize.** When we get to heaven, I believe the first question we will be asked is "whom did you bring with you?" Jesus' mission statement is "go and make disciples." If we call ourselves his followers, we can't avoid evangelizing—it is a core part of our identity in Christ.

3. **Pray. Then pray some more.** The hearts of others will be transformed only because of God's grace operating in their lives. Pray for others. Pray for yourself. Spiritual power depends on prayer. Our relationship with Christ is found in prayer.

4. **Support groups that are already doing good work.** If you know of such groups, invest in them and their great work in transforming culture. Invest your time. Invest your money. Don't let another opportunity pass to put your money where your beliefs are. And don't be fooled into thinking we can change culture through mere politics. Politics reflects where our culture has already gone. Finally, we must also affirm what is still good about our modern culture and try to support those things as well.

5. **Focus on youth and young adults.** Young people are not the future of the Church—they are already part of it, so we need to make sure they not only stay in the Church but help the Church grow and thrive. We can assure this happens by forming them and loving them. They will also be the primary evangelists (either for Jesus or the

culture) of the next generation. Time spent on forming disciples of young people is always time well spent.

6. **Learn how others have transformed culture in the past.** The negative changes in our culture didn't happen overnight, and neither will positive changes. We need to focus our efforts in areas such as the media, education, fine arts, and entertainment, offering positive alternatives when needed.

7. **Dream big.** Too many Catholics are fine with the status quo. But God dreams big and so should we. The entire world needs to be transformed. Where do we start? By taking the next step. I might add that we need to support our leaders when they do the right thing.

8. **Use all available tools, such as the Internet, new media, and other technologies.** Remember how the Industrial Revolution was driven by new technologies; such changes can be either negative or positive. The Church must always answer the "should we?" and "how should we if we do?" questions when it comes to progress.

9. **Stick to the basics.** Most modern people are basically unchurched or dechurched, even if they go to church sometimes. This means they know little (if anything) about a personal relationship with Jesus. The best place to start in reaching them is the Gospel message. Communicate it clearly and effectively.

10. **Invest time, energy, and talents in helping others.** The best way to transform culture is to help those we have influence with, such as children, spouses, other family members, friends, or coworkers Our best chance of

helping make positive changes lies within these relationships. Small changes can lead to cultural trends, so don't underestimate them.

11. **Our modern culture still has many good aspects.** Focus on those things and help to advance them. These include amazing medical advances (when done morally), ability to communicate in various ways cheaply and rapidly, access to information via the Internet and technology, more intercultural acceptance, and the ability to travel easily. Many other advances help our world as well. We need to make sure we focus on the positive and do not merely point out the negative.

Activities and Questions

1. Did you know the history of contraception, which preceded the sexual revolution? What do you think about it? Is it challenging to think that contraception is a bad thing?

2. Not everything about our modern culture is bad. List ten things that are good in our modern culture.

3. Practice one of the eleven ways to transform culture for the next few days. Which one is most attractive to you? Why?

CHAPTER 4

Strategies for Individuals Who Struggle with Porn

For once you were darkness, but now in the Lord you are light. Live as children of light. (Eph 5:8)

Before any young man joins an accountability group at our campus ministry, he must sit down with me and talk about the issue he is facing. We discuss many things, but I am mainly interested in knowing whether he's ready to make the essential changes in his life to stop using pornography and masturbating. A smaller percentage of students I see are in active sexual relationships outside of marriage. If the accountability group might benefit the student, I then tell him what he can look for in the group, and I answer any questions. If the group is not a good fit, I explain why.

After some months of being in the accountability group, a large percentage of young men decide to quit the group. Once I tell the students the realities of what they are facing, many of them discover they aren't ready to lose what has brought them so much misery. Even though most of them realize they will still have a lot of shame, hurt, and struggle, they choose porn over freedom from it. Many of them want a quick fix, and that almost never happens. Furthermore, many are looking for someone else to give them the perfect advice to make it all go away with little effort on their part. Most of these young men who walk away are not ready to address the situation. If you picked up this book hoping to find the silver bullet that would slay the problem you face, I am sorry to say there is none. You won't stop using porn easily.

Most people will struggle with lust and the allure of pornography for a long time. The average person who wants to stop using porn did not get hooked by just a few exposures to it, and most will not find freedom after only a few months of struggle. I have learned a difficult truth from the mental health professionals I have worked with: the recidivism rate is astronomical when it comes to sex addicts trying to quit their addiction. The high rate is due to the fact that sexual addiction is a brain disease and is not something the average addict will be able to stop quickly or on his own. This doesn't mean the cause is hopeless, but for most people this cross will be a burden for a while.

The difficulties and effort required, however, do not outweigh the benefits of living a life of virtue, holiness, and purity. Despite the bumpy road that many will have in trying to rid themselves of pornography, they will never regret choosing the better way. Being freed from the chains of addiction and being able to better love God and others is worth whatever the price. The outcome means a better and happier life. Finally, our heavenly reward will be even better than anything this earth can offer.

18 Strategies to Stop

STRATEGY 1: Get rid of all pornography and future access to it. For persons addicted to crack, for example, the first step of recovery is to get rid of the drugs in their presence and then keep them from future access. This means changing friendships, staying away from areas drug dealers frequent, ending relationships with other addicts, and possibly even moving. Once access and means to acquire the drugs are lessened or eliminated, the possibility of sobriety goes up. Similarly, you must destroy movies, magazines, and all electronic images having to do with porn. You must also restrict access to porn, so that in a moment of weakness (which is sure to come), you can limit the chances of accessing images you don't want to see. Blocking software must be put on all electronic devices (computer, phone, gaming systems, tablets, etc.). If you are smart enough to know how to bypass the blocks, you might even have to give up your computer. For a list of blocking software options, see the resources section of this book.

If you do keep your computer, keep it in a public spot. If for some reason you absolutely need access to a computer (for work or school), make sure you are always safe from the temptations that want to get at your soul. Use the computer in a public place and stay off of it while alone. If you have premium channels on cable, dump them (and maybe even cable altogether). Furthermore, because pornography on phones is so popular, you need to limit access to the Internet and pictures on your phone. Buy a simple phone (smart phones are trouble for sex addicts) and dump the tablet. These strategies will be difficult for those who are very plugged in. But if you find good and creative ways to fill the time you once spent on electronic devices, you will probably lead a more fulfilling life anyway.

STRATEGY 2: Find an accountability partner. Check in with each other frequently. Many will have a quick reaction to this suggestion—I don't want to tell anyone about this, much less depend upon someone else! I understand the reticence to lean on someone else, but your ability to have authentic relationships with others has been damaged. It's a bad thing to believe we can't depend on others for help. In fact, if true healing is to take place, then each person must strive for humility and openness in relationships. This means allowing others into the dark part of our lives and letting their love help us.

For men, the best accountability partner is another man who is a strong Christian and a prayerful brother in Christ. Similarly, women need another woman who follows Jesus first and who is willing to help. If you are married, dating, or engaged, I recommend not having your significant other be your accountability partner. This is because they need to seek their own healing and will not be able to be patient enough with your process of healing to offer what you need.

If you are not an addict but still struggle with lust, regular Confession and possibly separate meetings for pastoral counseling (with the same priest) might be enough. Another way of being accountable is to join a twelve-step group or a faith-based accountability group.

If you feel you are working yourself into a situation that you know you have little control over, then *stop* and reach out to your accountability partner. This is the moment you will need him or her most, so do this as quickly as possible.

You will find some principles and the basic structure of an accountability group in the resources section at the end of the book.

STRATEGY 3: If you are married, tell your spouse. If your spouse does not know about your problem, you need to talk about it. The problem must be admitted before it can stop. Many addicts hide their addiction due to the shame they feel. You must bring your problems into the light in order to overcome them. Hiding your sin and shame in the dark is exactly where the devil wants to keep you.

STRATEGY 4: Learn your triggers and develop an action plan to counter them. Most people struggle more with their sexuality at certain times and in certain places and situations. You will need to recognize when and where these temptations arise. For instance, many will masturbate in the shower, where they are alone and naked. If this is the case for you, plan on doing something different before entering the bathroom to avoid a bad situation in the shower. Maybe you will need to pray before entering, pray while you are showering, and take a short shower at an uncomfortable temperature. You may even have to avoid the shower if you start to feel tempted before you get in and you don't believe you could resist the temptation.

You also need to think about how you are feeling when strong temptations arise. Many people struggle most when they feel tired, stressed, bored, lonely, sad, or hurt. If you start to feel this way, you will need to learn new ways to deal with such feelings. Find healthy responses to feelings: prayer, calling a close friend or family member, exercising, or another activity.

Everyone has different triggers. Some use pornography and masturbate to release tension, to relax, or to deal with stress or problems. Once you identify a trigger, try to go beyond it to see what caused you to act.

Joe was very down after having a relapse months into his recovery. Once he explored what had happened, he uncovered an interesting chain of events that led him to act out. First he remembered looking at porn and masturbating. Before that he looked at Web sites that he knew featured women in bikinis. Before that he started to be tempted by thinking of the sex he had had years before with an old girlfriend. Before that he felt bored and lonely. Before that he was alone at home and had nothing to do for hours in between doing all his chores and waiting to go to a movie. Before that he was thinking about not having a girlfriend for the last year. Before that he was frustrated with work. Before that he remembered his boss coming down hard on him.

Joe realized that he had started to feel bad about himself and his status at work because his boss had strong words for him. That was the impetus behind it all. At any point where Joe recognized the trajectory toward porn, he could have made a better decision. When he was feeling bad about work, he could have prayed and made a decision to talk to his boss the next day. When he felt lonely, he could have gone for a walk or called a friend. When he started to think about his old girlfriend, he could have called his accountability partner to say he was feeling tempted. No matter where he was, he always had another decision to make. He could have made much better choices than the path he chose.

STRATEGY 5: Practice fasting. Fasting helps develop self-control and mastery over your desires. If you have had a problem with sexual self-control, chances are that you also have self-control issues in other areas. If you are to live a healthier and more integrated life, you will need to learn to make better choices. One way of doing this is to learn the benefit of fasting from food in a balanced and healthy way. Those who can do so will do much better in controlling their sexual compulsions.

Not only does fasting teach self-control, but it also helps us focus on what is truly important. Fasting helps unite us to the poor, reminds us of how blessed we are, and teaches us to be thankful for what we have. Furthermore, if we can offer our fasting for the intentions of others, it teaches us to be more selfless.

STRATEGY 6: Learn how to overcome the temptation. Below are seven Biblical ways to overcome temptation:

> ➢ Avoid and/or flee from it. Sometimes discretion is the better part of valor. Joseph fled when his master's wife tried to seduce him:
>
>> *"She caught hold of his garment, saying, 'Lie with me!' But he [Joseph] left his garment in her hand, and fled and ran outside" (Gen 39:12).*

> ➢ Submit your thoughts to God. He knows better than we do what is good.

"Finally, beloved, whatever is true, whatever is honorable, whatever is just, whatever is pure, whatever is pleasing, whatever is commendable, if there is any excellence and if there is anything worthy of praise, think about these things" (Phil 4:8).

➢ Overcome your selfishness. True love doesn't know selfishness. Because if you love Jesus, you don't belong to yourself.

"And you belong to Christ, and Christ belongs to God" (1 Cor 3:23).

➢ Expect and be ready for temptation. We need to be prepared for spiritual battle.

"Therefore take up the whole armor of God, so that you may be able to withstand on that evil day, and having done everything, to stand firm" (Eph 6:13).

➢ Remind yourself of the consequences of sin.

"Now the works of the flesh are obvious: fornication, impurity, licentiousness, idolatry, sorcery, enmities, strife, jealousy, anger, quarrels, dissensions, factions, envy, drunkenness, carousing, and things like these. I am warning you, as I warned you before: those who do such things will not inherit the kingdom of God" (Gal 5:19–21).

➢ Memorize helpful verses from God's word. Filling our minds with the thoughts of God and having them readily available to us is wise.

"But he said, 'Blessed rather are those who hear the word of God and obey it!'" (Lk 11:28).

➤ Cultivate a sense of God's presence. But don't just listen—obey.

> *"Go near, you yourself, and hear all that the* LORD *our God will say. Then tell us everything that the* LORD *our God tells you, and we will listen and do it"* (Deut 5:27).

STRATEGY 7: Use holy images. The mind of someone who has looked at porn over an extended period has thousands of ungodly images. Start to fill it with the image of Christ, Mary, and the saints. Many people surround their computer screens with holy cards. Others put an image of their favorite prayer on the wallpaper of their phone. Still others glue crosses to the back of a phone or carry one in their pocket as a reminder of their goal: freedom from porn. The point is to try and allow more room for good images and less for bad ones.

STRATEGY 8: Ask Mary to intercede. It's hard to be tempted when asking the Immaculate Mother of God to help you. Mary is the icon of what it means to be human. Though she must have been tempted, as Jesus was, the Church teaches that she never sinned. God gave her a unique gift of grace, and Mary was completely open to it. She didn't earn grace (otherwise it wouldn't have been grace), but she cooperated with the gift. We too stand in utter need of God. So ask Mary to help you to be open to God's grace, and ask her to pray for you. Allow her to be a model of purity, patience, love, and chastity. Permit our Blessed Mother to take you to her divine Son.

STRATEGY 9: Pray and read Scripture daily. Let God's word penetrate deeply into your life. Chapter 6 of this book is on prayer and the importance of developing a deep prayer practice to allow God profoundly into your life.

STRATEGY 10: Frequent the sacraments. Go to Confession often, to the same priest if possible. Go to Mass as often as you can.

STRATEGY 11: Do not suppress the thoughts of temptation. Redeem them. While it isn't healthy to entertain a tempting thought, Jesus can help us to overcome them when we are unable to do so ourselves. To redeem our temptations means we must offer them to Christ through his cross. When you are tempted, stop and pray to Jesus. You might say, "Jesus, I give you this temptation, which makes me feel drawn to act in a way that doesn't bring you glory. Help me to overcome this temptation by the power of your grace. Amen." Then you will need to focus your mind on something holy, such as a Bible verse you have memorized.

Too often we humans believe that we should be able to improve ourselves on our own. This is a cultural phenomenon of self-medication and self-improvement. But that's not the case with porn and other addictions; we can't do it on our own.

The first step of all twelve-step addiction recovery programs is to admit powerlessness over the addiction that the person is suffering from. The second is to believe that there is a higher power who can restore each person. The third is to choose to turn one's life and will over to God, who can help. This goes for sexual addicts as well. Only when we allow God into the sin, the pain, the shame, and the wounds is he able to free us from it all. We are not made to do things alone.

STRATEGY 12: Do not drink alcohol while trying to overcome the temptation. Drinking can lower inhibitions, which makes us more likely to act impulsively. A lot of bad things have happened because someone was tipsy, drunk, or high. A lack of self-control lurks at the heart of every addiction. Alcohol and drugs, like porn itself, only make you feel good for a short time. They never help solve the problems you are suffering from. Choose to stay away from alcohol for a while and from illegal drugs forever. Once you have gained self-control for a considerable period (I would suggest one year of being sexually sober), then you can return to drinking a very moderate amount of alcohol. (This presumes you follow the laws about age, and never drive after drinking.) Illegal drugs should never be used.

STRATEGY 13: Don't beat yourself up after a setback. The devil wants you to give up. Seek forgiveness and start again, no matter how humbling or hard it may be. God always forgives and loves. The devil will tell you many lies: You're no good. You can't do it. You aren't worth the effort. Nobody loves you. God doesn't care about you. You're too weak. Everybody is doing it. It will make it all better. It isn't so bad.

The truth is that if you fail, you will most likely feel bad; you may even feel horrible about yourself for a while. But to remain in this state is to allow the devil to keep you right where he wants you. He wants you to feel like a pig wallowing around in the muck, believing you aren't any good and can't ever get clean. Don't ever believe the lies of the devil. Make the choice to start over. Make the choice for yourself, your loved ones, and Jesus.

STRATEGY 14: Exercise regularly. Every one of us has physical desires that can be very strong. Sometimes it can feel as if our bodies are about to explode and we are no longer in full control. When this happens, usually hormones and energy have built up and are looking for release. Many find this release in masturbation and looking at porn.

A healthier way to release these hormones and use your body is to exercise vigorously. You could run, lift weights, play a sport, or engage in another activity. Whatever kind of exercise you choose, make sure you do it regularly and vigorously. Push yourself in a healthy way.

As with many other changes in habit, if you haven't been exercising regularly for a while, it will take time to get in the habit and to get in shape. Thus, having someone to exercise with can help. If you don't have a partner, you might consider joining a gym or club, which has built-in accountability for exercising. Set clear goals that will drive you but that you can still achieve.

You ought not start any major changes in exercising without making sure you are physically fit enough to do so. Before you get into running a marathon or tripling your strength, talk to your physician. Furthermore, you ought not push yourself to the point of exhaustion, and when you do push yourself, do so in slowly increasing ways.

STRATEGY 15: Practice custody of the eyes. To have custody of the eyes means we control what we look at and how we react to the things we see. Almost all those who use porn struggle with controlling where their eyes will fall on the body of someone they find attractive. Sometimes I see a man (or woman) looking someone up and down. When this happens, I stop and say a prayer for that person, knowing that in lusting after another, he or she lacks self-control.

All of us should practice custody of the eyes. Here are nine more reasons why:

1. It helps teach discipline. Discipline helps us control our passions and not allow them to control us.

2. It avoids the near occasion of sin. To avert your eyes when you feel tempted to use another person lustfully is a good thing.

   "But I say to you that everyone who looks at a woman with lust has already committed adultery with her in his heart" (Mt 5:28).

3. Custody of the eyes builds up chastity. If we do not have custody of the eyes, then our sexuality is disordered toward objectification—not love—and needs to be healed.

4. It is what every gentleman and lady should do. Nobody who respects himself or herself wants to be lusted after or looked up and down. No real gentleman or lady would dishonor another person by doing so.

5. It helps us to see the whole person, not just parts of a body.

   When most people see an immodestly dressed person, the manner of how they think of the other person can rapidly change. Thus, men need to be able to see the truth about who a woman is—not just break her down into objects he can use for his selfish pleasure and vice versa. Rather than lusting for someone, we should remind ourselves of the dignity of the person. That person is God's daughter or son, with the right to be loved (not lusted after), and is worthy of our respect.

6. It avoids scandal. In the Old Testament King David lusts after Bathsheba when he sees her nude while

bathing. He commits adultery with her and then has her husband killed to hide his sin. If he had practiced custody of the eyes he might have been able to avoid much worse sins—adultery and murder.

7. It helps fight off temptation. All suffer from some form of sexual temptation at some point. To have custody of the eyes helps fight off even stronger temptations.

8. It helps our sisters and brothers not feel objectified. If for no other reason, we should witness to the dignity of other human beings by controlling our passions. And though our sisters and brothers in Christ should also help by dressing modestly, even an immodestly dressed person is made to be loved.

9. It helps us focus on more important things. *"But strive first for the kingdom of God and his righteousness, and all these things will be given to you as well" (Mt 6:33).* Christ should be our first priority. Honoring the height of his visible creation (other humans) should be the second. We ourselves should be third.

STRATEGY 16: Spend time in service to others. This could be any sort of service, such as mowing an elderly neighbor's lawn, feeding the hungry in a soup kitchen, or helping someone with tax forms. What matters is to go out of your own world and serve others.

One of the consequences of using pornography is that it turns us inward. It makes us think only of our own selfish desires and worry about ourselves. When we regularly serve others, we start to overcome this turning inward by orienting ourselves to others. It also helps us appreciate our blessings and learn selfless love.

Finally, we are made to serve others, so it helps us find out what it means to truly be images of God, who pours himself out in love for us. Find a way to serve others this week—even put it on your calendar if necessary. But never forget that our first service to others should start at home. Never forget to serve your family first—in the ways they want you to love them, not just the ways you want to love them.

STRATEGY 17: Stay busy. One of the primary triggers for those who have a problem with porn is boredom or simply having too much time on their hands. Making sure you are busy keeps your mind from wandering. Most of those I have worked with say that physical labor is one of the best strategies. It tires them so they sleep better; it keeps them busy; and it keeps both the mind and body occupied. Regardless of what you do, make sure you aren't just "wasting time" but spending your time doing something of value. Writing down a list of possible things you can do and adding to it periodically can help. Refer to the list whenever you start to feel bored or tempted.

STRATEGY 18: Seek professional help. If you feel that despite your best efforts, you are unable to stop viewing pornography, find a mental health professional who specializes in addiction. He or she will be able to help you in ways that nobody else can. I highly suggest you find a Christian counselor who understands sexual addiction well.

None of these strategies alone will help you conquer all of your temptations. Also, you will have to constantly practice them even after you have started to regain self-control, because temptations can rise again if you let your guard down. The strategies are meant to be the first step in learning to live a life of virtue and happiness, and only by being virtuous can we live our lives to their full potential.

Activities and Questions

1. What strategies do you think would help you most? Why? Write down your answers and then discuss with your accountability group or partner.

2. Starting with the first strategy, work your way through them one at a time. You will need to work on some of them time and time again, while others are one-time events. Write a reminder somewhere, perhaps even on the back of your hand, to help you remember to practice the strategy you are working on.

3. Which strategy do you think would be the hardest for you? Why would it be so hard?

4. Do you feel motivated to work on your problems using these suggestions? Why or why not?

Chapter 5

Virtue Is Not a Dirty Word

For this very reason, you must make every effort to support your faith with goodness, and goodness with knowledge. (2 Pt 1:5)

Many sex addicts try to overcome their addiction on their own. Almost all of them discover it is virtually impossible for the average addict to stop the addiction without personal help. They are longing for true intimacy, love, and relationships that are good for them. They want to try and "fix" their own problems without having to lean on someone else. That is the wrong way to go about things.

Good friends aren't easy to find, neither is a good accountability partner for a sex addict. Accountability partners will usually become great friends, because they will hold each other accountable for their prayer life, decisions, and sexuality. They will need to talk frankly about their struggles and their common desire to grow closer to God. What really helps them is the freedom of letting down their guard around each other, because ultimately they should want the same thing: to grow in holiness.

To discover what it means to be free from porn is to discover deep hope, charity, patience, perseverance, chastity, humility, and temperance. It also means that accountability partners should forge a bond of friendship built on being able to trust and help each other.

All sex addicts have to constantly remain on guard (for the rest of their lives) against their own fallen nature, the attacks of the enemy, and the temptations to abuse their sexuality. But through a patient and faithful friend and with the help of much grace, they can find freedom from the chains of porn. To do this, each person must work on building up virtue while holding the other accountable for working on himself.

Fake It Until You Make It!

Our ultimate goal is to achieve sexual purity and chastity, which are virtues. Virtue is the habit that steers us toward doing what is right and good. Once it has become a habitual part of our life, virtue becomes an easy choice. But developing any virtue will be difficult and take time. Until then, good decisions still need to be worked on. Ancient philosophers and Catholic theologians have taught that the most prudent way to build a virtue is to act as if we already possess it. Over time, when we act as if we possess a virtue, we will eventually develop it.

In other words, if I want to be patient, I act as if I am patient, even if it is hard to do so. In the same way, if I want to be chaste and pure, I need to act as if I am. I have to fake it until I make it.

There are two kinds of virtues: those that are supernatural, which means they are not part of our nature and are infused in our souls by the grace given us at Baptism (and strengthened in us by Confirmation), and those that we acquire in natural ways by practicing them. Faith, hope, and love are supernatural virtues. They are also traditionally called the three theological virtues, because they are given by God without our meriting them. On the other hand many virtues are acquired through practicing them on the natural level. These include patience, chastity, humility, temperance, and perseverance.

Faith

Faith is a supernaturally infused virtue that first gives us the gift of knowing about God and then the ability to choose to believe in him. Although we can open ourselves up to receiving the gift of faith by following our right reason and by choosing to act in a good way, we cannot grow our faith on our own. It is always a gift from God. It allows our intellect to understand supernaturally revealed truths that we cannot figure out by ourselves. For instance, belief in the doctrine of the Trinity is a gift from God, because God has revealed it to us and we assent to the belief through faith.

Naturally, we can gain knowledge through our senses and intellect. But all those things above and beyond this sensory knowledge must be gained by faith. Thus, when we believe Jesus is God and that by his death and resurrection we can have life eternal, we have been given a grace we cannot acquire naturally.

In terms of being faithful to God in our sexuality, we must believe that because we are made in God's image and likeness, we have a higher purpose and a responsibility to act a certain way. Thus, faithfully living out our sexuality means we must follow God's plan for us and believe it is better than our own.

Hope

Hope is not optimism, which is a sentimental feeling that things generally are fine. Hope, rather, is an anchor to the soul (see Heb 6:19). It provides vigor and life, because it rests in the promise of our eternal destiny and the love of our Lord. Hope isn't built upon our own power, but rather on the cornerstone of our faith: Jesus Christ. We know that he has conquered death and sin, though we still struggle with both.

Hope rests our eyes on heaven, while optimism keeps our eyes on the earth. Hope is founded in God, whereas optimism is founded in our own strength and feelings. To conquer sexual sin and truly open our hearts to God requires God's grace and the virtue of hope. Persons who have hope need not rely on their own strength, but know that God will always keep his promises to love and help us. While this may not make the journey to heaven less bumpy, it helps us remain faithful and loving while persevering through the trials of life.

Despair is the vice opposed to hope. When we despair, we lose the life that is in our soul. Despair is thus a thief that robs us of the ability to see beyond the reality of our present situation. Hope, instead, gives us the eyes to see heaven as our future and God's strength resting in our souls.

Hope is the virtue that balances faith and love. If you struggle to love, but believe in God, hope is the impetus that can help you move from mere belief to loving action. On the other hand, if you struggle to believe, yet love, hope is that impetus that can help move that love into believing in the promises our God makes.

Love and Charity

People have many false ideas of "true love." Some equate love with sex. Others believe that love is all about falling "in love" and that it depends on our emotional state. But to understand what love is really all about, we have to learn from the one who is love itself: Jesus. Think of the stories of Jesus' life—he never failed to love. Christ loved us to the point of suffering torture, humiliation, scourging, mocking, betrayal, and a horrible death on a cross. We are called to nothing less than this kind of self-giving love. A true follower of Jesus must aspire to such love. Yet this kind of love is foreign to people today, and an evangelizer must make a concerted effort to teach about it.

This kind of love is charity, which isn't merely giving to the needy. Charity is loving God for God's sake and loving our neighbor because we first love God.

We can practice this kind of love every day. When I was growing up I used to hate doing the dishes because I was required to do them. After I got married, I continued to dislike doing the dishes and I would take every chance to avoid doing them. It dawned on me one day—through the grace of God— that by acting that way, I was failing to love my wife and, in turn, failing to love God. So I decided that from that day forward I would make it my desire to do the dishes. That doesn't mean that I immediately enjoyed doing them, but my perspective changed. Instead of trying to get out of a chore, I saw it as a chance to love my wife and God by dying to my own desires. My wife is certainly happier with my attitude about the dishes!

Beneath this attitude change was a paradigm shift at a deeper level. While I loved my wife and others, in certain ways I was unconsciously acting as if they only existed to serve me. Thus, I needed to adjust my conscious attitude about how I was called to love. As I have already pointed out, using another person as a means to an end is the opposite of true love. When my head realized what I was doing, my heart started to change. It's not that I have perfected this charitable kind of love, but my mind and heart are properly oriented now, so I have the opportunity to love more humbly, selflessly, and fruitfully.

To love and be loved is the greatest human desire. We are made out of love, by love, for love, in order to love. When we choose love, we start to live for our deepest purpose and desire. We find true meaning in our lives—even though it isn't necessarily easy or natural to us all the time. The virtue of charity is a great gift, but this gift comes with assembly required.

Patience

The one virtue I don't like to pray for is patience. Inevitably, God will quickly answer my prayer by giving me several opportunities to practice patience. In these situations I have to struggle to be patient. I might get stuck in traffic after a tiring day of work, or have to wait a long time to be served at a restaurant when I'm very hungry. Although these situations work for my ultimate good, it still isn't easy because I don't have the virtue of patience yet.

The same is true for any other virtue. We have to struggle with it. But in the struggle we will learn to rely on God's grace and allow his power to be the force that keeps us moving forward toward virtue.

We sometimes believe we should be healed and completely virtuous right now! We don't like waiting for change to happen, because change is hard. So we become impatient. But it's good not only to pray for patience, but also to look for opportunities to practice it. For example, you could delay something you want. When you are very thirsty after going for a run, wait thirty seconds before drinking a big glass of water. While doing so, ask God to help you grow in patience and in gratitude. These small acts add up.

Chastity

In working with young men, I have found that very few have developed the virtue of chastity. Most of them don't even understand it. How can they become chaste if they don't understand the goal they are aiming for?

Most people who do not understand the virtues confuse chastity and celibacy. Celibacy is the choice to refrain from sexual activity. It can be because someone is single, a priest, or a religious sister or brother. Because the person is not married, he or she chooses to not have sex.

Chastity is rightly ordering your sexuality to your station in life. This means that everyone—single, religious, priests, and married—is called to be chaste, but in different ways. A married couple's chastity means they have sex with each other, but not that "anything goes." For those who are not married, chastity means refraining from all sexual activity.

The virtue of chastity allows us to give ourselves to another. Love can be defined as a gift of yourself to another. To give yourself to your spouse means you give everything—there is no selfishness in that love. Chastity is the virtue that frees our love from sexual selfishness and allows us to love our spouses and God completely, without being a slave to our sexual desires.

Chastity means freedom: freedom from lust, freedom to love, freedom to be the persons God created us to be. Chastity has a bad rap in our culture. It is often dismissed as being prudish or as repressing one's sexuality. Don't buy the lies! We were made for chastity because we were made for love.

Humility

Humility is another misunderstood virtue. It does not mean thinking that we are no good. Rather, humility means to properly understand who God is and who we are in relation to God. God gives us certain gifts and blessings. We must recognize our nothingness before God and make sure that we do not credit ourselves for our gifts.

But it would be a false humility to think too little of ourselves. When we believe that we are unlovable, unforgivable, or no good at all, this is not humility but pride. Many people who struggle with their sexuality struggle with this kind of pride.

A proper understanding of who we are helps us to see the beauty that God has put within us. But we know this beauty is all because of him and not because of our own abilities. Christ showed us true humility by becoming one of us.

Perseverance

If you have ever mastered a musical instrument, you know what perseverance is. Perseverance is required when a clarinet sounds like a herd of hamsters being squeezed. Perseverance gets marriage through hard times and Navy Seals through training. It is the virtue that keeps us going even when we want to quit. It enables us to seek the good, no matter how hard it is to reach it.

Those who struggle with pornography will inevitably struggle with persevering in that battle. Yet to overcome pornography, we will need to find the strength to overcome it. This strength doesn't come from our own nature, but is a grace from God. We don't earn it. We don't deserve it. But we have it nonetheless. To tap into the grace of God, we must develop the inner strength of character that gets us through the tough times. Fasting is one practice that helps foster the virtue of perseverance. By limiting the natural desires of our body in one area, we can learn to do the same in our sexuality.

Temperance

Temperance is often thought of only as a virtue related to drinking alcohol. While that is one way to practice temperance, it certainly isn't the only way. Temperance is the virtue of not seeking too much of something that is good or morally neutral. In other words, it helps us moderate our passions. These passions could be alcohol, food, and other desires, but in the context of porn, it means we temper our desire for sex.

Temperance is related to many other virtues, including chastity. Temperance helps us to control the desires of the flesh in a reasonable way. This means we abstain from fulfilling certain desires, when appropriate. In and of itself, temperance does not lead to lasting happiness, but it can help us to avoid sin. It also helps us find happiness, because it allows us to enjoy good things in a reasonable way.

Activities and Questions

1. Pick a virtue that you want to work on and start to fake it until you make it. Try to work on it for the next two months.

2. What are one or two virtues you believe you already have by nature? How did you acquire it (them)?

3. Think of someone you know who has a virtue you find difficult to practice. How does that virtue make that person's character or personality attractive? Why does that attract you?

CHAPTER 6

The Necessity of Prayer, Penance, and the Sacraments

Devote yourselves to prayer. (Col 4:2)

Knowing Your Story

If you are addicted to pornography, remember the time before your addiction started and ask yourself these questions: What first led me to porn? Why I was first attracted to it? Was I trying to compensate for or cover up any emotional wound, abuse, pain, or brokenness in my family? What was I looking for when I turned to porn? What has my porn addiction brought me in my life?

Understanding what happened in our past and where we are today can help us start to heal from the wounds and issues porn has caused. Many porn addicts will only find healing with aid from a counselor who can help probe these issues. Of course, many will make excuses as to why they shouldn't or can't see a counselor. If you think that, then ask yourself another question: What am I willing to sacrifice to overcome the problem? If the sacrifice doesn't include money, time, effort, prayer, pride, pleasure, and so forth, then you may not be able to stop by yourself. This means you will need professional help, which will cost time and money anyway.

Most porn addicts have some underlying problem that led to porn. This root problem must be dealt with to help the person find freedom. The problems are many, and each person has unique issues. No matter what might have led to a life of using pornography, know that you can always find grace, freedom, and peace in Jesus. Porn can never give us what we are truly looking for, which is found only in a life spent with our God.

Porn will never satisfy. It always leaves us demanding more. It will never bring us the happiness and peace we are looking for. Jesus always satisfies and only asks us to give him our hearts. Porn is a mistress who will never deliver what is promised. Jesus is the lover who will always fulfill the promises he makes to us. Through all the struggles we may face, we bring our temptations, brokenness, sin, and successes to Jesus in prayer.

Ultimately, prayer life will need transformation. Once we pour our lives into Jesus, through prayer, we can find what we need. All of us come to him as sick patients who need the medicine of his grace. Prayer is the foundation on which to build a relationship with the Divine Physician. In this relationship we receive our cure: Jesus himself.

Praying Badly

All of us have difficulties with prayer. Because prayer is a relationship, it takes a lot of work just to get to the point of being okay. Many of us start out by basing our prayers on good experiences and emotions. As in a romantic relationship, this basis is good because it helps bring two beings closer together. But real love must also be fostered once we stop relying on emotional highs and great experiences. Once the emotions leave, we must decide to love the other person for his or her own sake, not what that person can do for us. Real love is choosing what is best for another regardless of what it costs.

This kind of love isn't easy. Sometimes you will feel far from God and that your prayer is dry or boring. But you are not alone. Seek the help of a good spiritual director or confessor. You also need to continue to pray even when it doesn't feel good to do so. This is a sign of true love for God—to choose to pray, even when you may not want to, because you know it is the best thing to do. If you continue to pray, your faith will grow beyond the feelings.

Although these dry times may not feel like a gift from God, they truly are. They give us the opportunity to go beyond our feelings and develop a true, loving relationship with God. We shouldn't waste such an opportunity!

Think of it this way: what would be more pleasing to God—twenty minutes of easy prayer with great emotions, or twenty minutes in which we struggle with dryness, don't want to pray, yet persevere anyway? I would say the second, because we choose to do it even though we don't want to. God is pleased with the times we choose him, especially when it is difficult, no matter how the prayer feels to us.

How Are You Doing?

I once asked a class of college students to rate their spiritual lives on a scale of one to ten. Most were very hard on themselves and gave themselves a five or less. I then asked them: "How would you describe your relationship with God?" Again, most were not very positive. When I asked them why, most of them said it was because of difficulties in prayer. Why do we have such difficulties? Simple—we are human. But before I offer some tips on how to overcome difficulties, let's talk about why we pray. Saint Paul writes, "Pray in the Spirit at all times in every prayer and supplication" (Eph 6:18).

Paul doesn't just suggest but commands us to pray "in the Spirit" at "all times." We should do this out of love, not out of mere obedience. But how are we to meet this high call? Paul writes: "Likewise the Spirit helps us in our weakness; for we do not know how to pray as we ought, but that very Spirit intercedes with sighs too deep for words" (Rom 8:26).

We can't do it alone. The Holy Spirit does for us what we can't do in our prayer. This is vital, because prayer is essential for success. I mean success in the eyes of God, which is much different from success by the world's standards. If you want to stop using pornography, that would be a spiritual success. The world sees success in terms of temporal things like money, fame, power, possessions, or pleasure. God's idea of success is holiness —being the person God made you to be. In other words, success is fulfilling the vision for your life that God has for you. To achieve that, prayer is indispensable.

Luke writes in his Gospel, "Then Jesus told them a parable about their need to pray always and not to lose heart" (Lk 18:1). We must make prayer the center of our lives. It isn't optional for us as Christians. But it requires perseverance and faith to achieve such a prayer life. In fact, I believe a good part of the answer to the question, "Do you have a personal relationship with Jesus?" can be answered by pointing to your prayer life. If you pray a good amount every single day, then you have a personal relationship with Jesus. But if you don't pray, you can't tap into the spiritual power needed to overcome the problems in your life, especially deep-seated issues such as a sex addiction. With this in mind, you might ask: Why would any Christian let prayer life slip? What can we do about it?

7 Reasons We Let Our Prayer Lives Slip

1. **Discouragement**. Sometimes we don't know what to say, how to pray, or what to do. Sometimes we are tired, feeling bad, or just don't have a desire to pray. Many of us then get discouraged and ask whether prayer matters and why we should do it.

2. **Doubt**. Is God really there? Can he hear me? Does he care, even if he exists? Does prayer really even matter? Doubts are a part of life. But faith can overcome doubts when we decide to choose to believe and follow Jesus.

3. **Impatience**. Although prayer can seem to go on forever, it may meet only with silence from heaven. When will God answer me? We chafe at God's timetable when it doesn't match our own. When we believe the world should operate according to our plans, we can become impatient with God's plan and our inability to understand it all.

4. **Temptations.** It is easy to pray when we aren't challenged internally through temptation. But when temptations arise, prayer becomes drudgery. How many sex addicts have stopped praying, or never dedicated themselves to prayer, because they don't see how a "sinner" could connect to God? But Jesus didn't come to save those who are already perfect. He came to help the sick and those who are suffering. He came to save the sinner. He came to save you and me.

5. **Laziness.** We sometimes give up or never establish habits that sustain us in dry times or through the busyness of modern life. If you are like me, you may be a procrastinator. I can be very lazy, and that goes for my prayer life too. Without real goals and the resolution to follow through, laziness can cause us to stop praying.

6. **Dryness.** When God seems distant, prayer becomes a chore. This can happen at any time to any person. Sometimes it happens through our own fault, when we don't put effort into our prayer. It may also be due to something out of our control. A death in the family, a sudden job loss, or an illness can make it feel as if God is far away. Often dryness occurs without any apparent reason, yet it is still difficult to deal with.

7. **Physical, mental, or emotional problems.** When we suffer it is hard to pray, because we sometimes think that a loving God would make it stop. We can react to suffering in three different ways. We can dive deeper into prayer, maintain the status quo, or let our prayer lives slip. Unfortunately, at the rough spots in life many people decide to stop praying.

15 Tips to Help Your Prayer Life

1. **Frequent the sacraments.** If you can make it to Mass even once a week besides Sunday Mass, you have doubled your access to the greatest gift ever given humanity. If you can go to Confession at least monthly, you will set yourself up for spiritual success and will surely receive many graces. If you have struggled to receive the sacraments frequently, try putting them on a calendar so you don't skip them. The sacraments are our lifeline, thrown to earth from heaven. Don't ever stop hanging on to them!

2. **Establish good habits.** Good habits can greatly help us in prayer. If you can commit to a routine of prayer for at least two months, you will start to lay the groundwork for healthy prayer habits. Also, don't try to do too much too soon. Prayer habits can be difficult to establish, so you want to succeed in sticking to them. Setting huge goals will make it seem impossible, so set smaller goals you know you can achieve.

3. **Accountability counts.** You need someone who is more objective than you are to look at your prayer life and see how the Holy Spirit is working. Many people who are struggling with their sexuality may not be ready for a spiritual director. But a Christian mentor is invaluable. Spiritual direction is primarily for those who aren't dealing with a major issue but are trying to grow in prayer. If you don't think you are ready for spiritual direction, it's good to have a Christian friend to talk to about prayer.

4. **Try different types of prayer**. We all have different tastes in prayer, just as in most other things in life. Try different types of prayer and see which ones work for you. One caveat: don't give up too soon on a type of prayer. It may take a long time to discover whether it is working for you. It doesn't matter if it is praying the rosary, praying with Sacred Scripture, praying the Liturgy of the Hours, or some other form of prayer. If you don't know where to start, ask your pastor or another person whose prayer life you admire.

5. **Fast regularly**. Fasting has great power, especially for overcoming pornography and other self-control problems. When we have better control over our bodily desires, we can pray better. Furthermore, starting to gain self-control over one of our natural desires (to eat) can help us learn to control other natural desires, including our desire for sex.

6. **Overcome distractions**. To overcome a distraction in prayer, simply turn your heart and mind back to your prayer. Don't even stop to think about the distraction. This is the easiest way to defeat it. Moreover, if you ever have a sexual thought while praying, simply thank God for your sexuality and again invite Jesus into your heart, while redirecting your mind to your prayer.

7. **Don't over-think prayer**. Too often we complicate what should come naturally to us. We are made for relationship and communion with God, who created us. Prayer is directing our mind and heart to God. If we over-complicate it, we tend to get caught up in the externals —what we are doing during prayer, the way we "ought"

to do it, and so on. We are human, and like every other human, we aren't going to pray perfectly.

8. **Realize that dryness can be good for us.** Dry prayer may be a gift from God. Yes, we all long to have consolations (the good feelings and easiness of praying), just as those with a sweet tooth long for candy. When the craving is denied, we won't like it and will find it difficult, but it is still healthy for us. During dryness our faith is tested and strengthened. When we are faithful to prayer despite dryness, we show the depth of our love for God.

9. **Pray for humility.** God's grace has power to change our lives to the extent that we are humble. Without humble prayer, God is unable to reach us, because we think we have no interior need for him. Humility isn't thinking we are no good. Rather, it is a proper understanding of who we are and who God is. We are not perfect, but we are still loved and gifted. All depends on our Lord because we live in utter need of God.

10. **Work on a proper understanding of God and self.** I cannot emphasize this enough. Many of us struggle to understand how a perfect God could love us and want a relationship with us. But we struggle because we don't understand our own dignity and the way God loves us unconditionally. Our sin, imperfections, and history are never barriers to God's love for us. He loves us despite those things, which is why his love is merciful—we don't deserve it.

11. **Be quiet.** Our modern lives are filled with noise. To hear God we need to quiet ourselves, both internally and externally. Find a peaceful and quiet place to pray. It's

helpful to stop at a church or set up a quiet location in your home where you can pray, even for a short time. We are persons with bodies and souls. One will affect the other. To quiet your body helps to quiet your soul.

12. **Prioritize prayer**. Schedule it. Bump something else. Get up early. Do whatever you have to do, but don't let a day go by without spending time with the most important person in your life. When we fail to pray, we fail to prioritize God in our lives. By our lack of prayer we allow other things to be more important than our Lord.

13. **Don't be too hard on yourself**. Struggles in your prayer life do not make you a terrible Christian. Everyone who prays has to struggle with it. Don't get down on yourself for your struggles. Realize that your life is an ongoing adventure and that God doesn't expect you to pray perfectly right now.

14. **Don't wait to start**. Procrastination is the enemy of prayer. If you feel called to pray, don't put it off. If you are asked to pray for someone else, stop and say a short prayer immediately. If you want a better prayer life, start now. Put down this book and pray. Make a resolution—and write it down—when you will pray daily and for how long. Later on you can figure out what you will do in your prayer.

15. **Find and use good resources**. If you don't know where to start with prayer, what to do, or how to do it, good resources can help. These include Sacred Scripture, wise and prayerful people in your life, friends who pray daily, books on prayer and spirituality, Web sites, or using sacramentals such as rosaries or statues as aids to prayer.

A Personal Relationship with Jesus

When my wife and I were dating, I wanted to spend as much time as I could with her. Why? Because I wanted to know her personally. I wanted to know what she liked and what she didn't. I wanted to get to know her pet peeves and her passions—everything about her. But above all else, I made the choice to love her.

When you love someone, you want the relationship to be as close, intimate, and personal as possible (appropriate to the kind of relationship, of course). The same goes with Jesus. All of us are called to a close, intimate, and personal relationship with Jesus. Of course, when it comes to a relationship with Jesus, we must always realize that before we ever act, he has acted first. The story of our relationship is not nearly as much about us pursuing him as his pursuing us. Still, if you are not sure where to start, try the following.

STEP 1: In any relationship, you choose how close you want to be with someone. Only you can make that choice. Your parents can initiate you into the faith through baptism. But once you get old enough, you have to choose faith for yourself, your parents can't do it for you. Nor can the Church as a whole. Many Catholics (and other Christians) have merely an intellectual or emotional connection to God, but not a personal one they have chosen in faith. To intellectually know Jesus (I know about Jesus) or have a movement of the emotions (I feel good about Jesus) isn't enough. Remember that even the demons know about Jesus and that we will all have times we don't feel good about Jesus ("take up your cross"). This is why we must *choose* Jesus in faith, which is done through an act of our will.

STEP 2: Once you choose Jesus in faith, you have to do it again and again. It isn't a one-time deal. This relationship is lived out primarily in prayer, the sacraments, growing in virtue (primarily love of God and others), and service to God and others—the many areas covered in this book. Jesus is Lord of all, and as servants to our King, we must serve him and others. This is what he commands us to do.

Some Catholics find this concept of a personal relationship with Jesus sounds too Protestant. That simply isn't true; it is an entirely Catholic concept. We were using the language long before our Protestant brothers and sisters. The universal Church has never lost touch with this language, even if some individuals or communities have. Here are some examples.

Pope Francis has said:

> Let the risen Jesus enter your life, welcome him as a friend, with trust: he is life! If up till now you have kept him at a distance, step forward. He will receive you with open arms. If you have been indifferent, take a risk: you won't be disappointed. If following him seems difficult, don't be afraid, trust him, be confident that he is close to you, he is with you and he will give you the peace you are looking for and the strength to live as he would have you do.[1]

The *Catechism of the Catholic Church* says: "This mystery [of faith], then, requires that the faithful believe in it, that they celebrate it, and that they live from it in a vital and personal

---

1. Francis (Homily on Holy Saturday, March 30, 2013), http://w2.vatican.va/content/francesco/en/homilies/2013/documents/papa-francesco_20130330_veglia-pasquale.html.

relationship with the living and true God. This relationship is prayer." [2]

In my wedding vows, when I promised that I would love my wife, I didn't make merely an emotional act (although emotions did play a part and there is nothing wrong with that). I didn't claim that I knew a lot about her (though I did, and that is good). Rather, I chose to love my wife that day and for always. Every time I choose to love her again, I affirm that initial commitment I made in my vows. The same is true for my relationship with Jesus. This is how you have a personal relationship with Jesus—you choose to do so again and again.

A close, intimate, and personal relationship with Jesus doesn't happen by accident. It must be intentional. Just as I was intentional about loving my wife when I made my vows, so we must all be intentional about following Jesus. The Bible certainly reflects that we must choose this relationship as well.

"Choose this day whom you will serve . . . as for me and my household, we will serve the LORD" (Jos 24:15).

"See, now is the acceptable time; see, now is the day of salvation" (2 Cor 6:2).

Activities and Questions

1. Write down three concrete goals to improve your prayer life over the next few months. If possible, find an accountability partner or a group to help you stick to them.

---

2. *Catechism of the Catholic Church*, no. 2558.

2. What kind of prayer appeals to you most? Why?

3. Stop and think about God. What images come to mind? How do these images reflect the truth about God? Do they reflect anything false? If so, how can you purify your understanding of God?

4. Have you ever stopped praying? If so, why? What would or did motivate you to start again?

5. Saint Thomas Aquinas is a patron of those seeking to live a chaste life. Here is a prayer he wrote asking for chastity.

> Dearest Jesus! I know well that every perfect gift, and above all others that of chastity, depends upon the most powerful assistance of your Providence, and that without you a creature can do nothing. Therefore, I pray that you defend, with your grace, the gift of chastity and purity in my soul as well as in my body. And if I have ever received through my senses any impression that could stain my chastity and purity, I ask you, who are the supreme Lord of all my powers, to take it from me, so that I may with a clean heart advance in your love and service, offering myself chaste all the days of my life on the most pure altar of your divinity. Amen.

CHAPTER 7

Protecting Your Home, Children, and Family from Porn

Now if you are unwilling to serve the LORD, choose this day whom you will serve, whether the gods your ancestors served in the region beyond the River or the gods of the Amorites in whose land you are living; but as for me and my household, we will serve the LORD. (Jos 24:15)

The Harmful Effects of Porn

Porn has a negative impact not only on families and individuals, but also on the wider culture. Every time someone looks at pornography, that person commercializes sex and objectifies other people. This fuels a mindset that sees sex as selfish, on-demand, and violent, denigrating others, especially women.

Think of commercials, pop music, sitcoms, movies, and other aspects of popular culture. They now portray a mindset that assumes pornography is culturally acceptable and used by all. The rapid acceptance of this mindset has trivialized sex and made it about selfishness and pleasure. The bonding of a couple (marriage doesn't even matter anymore) and the children that might result from having sex are now thought to be barriers to a good sex life. The deeper meaning of sex is not even considered.

From both aspects of making porn and using it, porn makes us see other persons as less than human. *Porn hurts others.* In our mind's eye we treat those involved in porn as objects for our pleasure, not as other people for whom we truly want what is best. This is the opposite of love. Although other human beings are the highest of visible creation, porn uses them as objects, not as persons of eternal worth and dignity.

The growth, accessibility, and ease of using porn have fueled a rapid growth in the sex trade. If we try to fight sexual slavery, trafficking, and exploitation while the demand for these things grows due to pornography, we will never get to the root of the problems. Porn drives the demand. Someone is sexually used to make porn—every time. Sometimes that person is a real-life slave.

Think of porn as the conduit that allows access to sexual exploitation. It conditions the users to objectify sex and become more desensitized to violence and aggression. Harmful attitudes and violence rapidly increase after repeated viewings of criminal acts such as rape and murder that are made to seem normal.

The porn industry doesn't want you to know this. Neither does the devil. They want you to believe porn is harmless. Lying, they say porn has no connection to social justice. They are wrong.

Those who are free from these lies need to bring the truth into the light. Sexual exploitation and trafficking begin in the homes of all those who choose to look at porn.

Our culture cannot recapture a true vision of humanity while pornography is a cultural norm.

Porn Destroys Relationships

According to the *Journal of Adolescent Health*, prolonged exposure to pornography leads to the following problems:[1]

➤ An exaggerated perception of sexual activity in society;

➤ Diminished trust between intimate couples;

➤ Abandoning the hope of sexual monogamy;

➤ Belief that promiscuity is the natural state;

➤ Belief that abstinence and sexual inactivity are unhealthy;

➤ Cynicism about love or the need for affection between sexual partners;

➤ Belief that marriage is sexually confining;

➤ Lack of attraction to family and child raising.

---

1. Dolf Zillmann, "Influence of Unrestrained Access to Erotica on Adolescents' and Young Adults' Dispositions toward Sexuality," *Journal of Adolescent Health*, vol. 27:2 (August 2000): 41–44.

With these problems, a spouse may often feel inferior to the images that the other spouse is using. Both partners suffer from self-esteem issues that distort their view of one another. No one can live up to the fantasy.

According to sociologist Jill Manning, research indicates that pornography consumption is associated with the following six trends,[2] among others:

1. Increased marital distress, and risk of separation and divorce;

2. Decreased marital intimacy and sexual satisfaction;

3. Infidelity;

4. Increased appetite for more graphic types of pornography and sexual activity associated with abusive, illegal, or unsafe practices;

5. Devaluation of monogamy, marriage, and child-rearing;

6. An increasing number of people who struggle with compulsive and addictive sexual behavior.

Porn also desensitizes the user with repeated use, numbing the conscience and opening the way to much deeper problems. Once desensitized to the serious nature of porn, a person will be open to much graver evils that hurt others even more deeply and directly. A proper sensitivity to pornography helps us set good boundaries around ourselves.

---

2. Jill C. Manning, "The Impact of Internet Pornography on Marriage and the Family: A Review of the Research" (Testimony before the U.S. Senate, Washington, DC, Nov. 10, 2005).

Protecting Your Home and Children

Tragically, pornography is easily accessible in most homes in our country. Too often parents rationalize the easy access and lack of barriers to porn in their home. Other times they don't put up barriers for their children because they themselves are using pornography regularly. Still others are naive about the extent of the problem.

Here are twelve ways you can protect your home and children from porn.

1. Use strict filtering software on your internet. Most homes now have a Wi-Fi network, which means you need to block porn from entering your home from the router, not just on your devices. Another device that lacks filtering software can use your Internet hookup to find porn.

2. Know where your kids are and with whom. Have honest conversations with those who are in charge of your children. Many kids will have their first encounter with porn away from home. Others will develop sexual habits outside of the home. Remember that even if your kids don't have a data plan on their phones, many of their friends probably do. It only takes one friend who says, "look at this" to start someone on a porn habit.

3. Model and teach your children appropriate physical affection. I give each of my kids a big hug and kiss several times a day. All of us yearn for appropriate physical affection. A hug means a lot. A lack of hugs means a lot, too. If you struggle with affection, challenge yourself to form a habit of modeling this for your children. If you

don't show them your love through affection, they might seek it in unhealthy ways.

4. Have regular dialogues with your children where they feel safe about asking questions. Forget about having a "birds and bees talk" in your house, because if you only talk about it once, you aren't helping your kids much. Rather, have many conversations about all kinds of topics. Include sexuality as one area of discussion, when fitting and in age-appropriate ways.

5. Make sure you establish suitable boundaries in your family regarding sexuality. Don't talk about the dangers of porn and then allow your kids to watch R-rated movies when they are fifteen. Talk about other people in a respectful way, and never make unfitting sexual comments about them.

6. Let your children know where you stand on the issue of pornography and teach them about its destructive nature. This should only be done at an age where children can properly discern the truth about sexuality. As much as we want to protect our kids from the damage of porn, neither do we want to tarnish the innocence of a young child. This decision must be left to the parents' discretion, because each child is different.

7. Expect and confirm your children's curiosity about sex. Don't chastise or punish them for this curiosity, but direct it into healthy actions. All kids are made for relationships, intimacy, and love, just like you and me. So be gentle with them when they do or say something that might push proper boundaries. At the same time, parents must balance this with a prudent understanding of

when punishment is properly warranted for more egregious violations of rules or standards.

8. Have open discussions about sexuality, culture, and issues your children may be concerned about. When they hear a bad word at school, don't overreact. When they bring home a friend who tries to get them to look under the door while a sibling is changing clothes, don't freak out. When they see a headline about sex trafficking while you are reading the paper, use it as a teaching moment when possible.

9. Help your children learn to tackle their feelings when tough situations arise in their lives. Most people who have a problem with porn don't know how to deal with painful emotions. This is especially true for situations that involve stress, anger, sadness, frustration, fatigue, and loneliness. Your children are not born with the ability to deal with all these situations. Help them learn by showing them healthy ways to deal with these situations and feelings, as well as modeling for them.

10. Always know more than your children do about the technology being used in your home. This is one of my goals as a dad—to be more tech-savvy than my kids while they are in my house. Some of you might struggle with this. If you aren't a tech guru, that is okay. But you should at least know enough about technology so you can protect your kids from themselves or others.

11. Monitor when and how your children use technology in your home. Do "mommy and daddy audits" periodically. Without warning, I go through the texts on my teenage daughter's phone (she doesn't have a data plan

yet). Her friends know I do this and so far we have never had an issue.

12. If your child is looking at porn already, seek professional help. Don't hesitate to do so or believe in cultural taboos regarding counseling. Your kid is worth whatever it might cost.

Activities and Questions

1. If porn has affected your relationships with your family, friends, and others, describe its effects.

2. What do you want to change about these relationships?

3. Have you been proactive about protecting your home from porn? If so, in what ways? If not, how can you improve?

CHAPTER 8

What to Do If
Your Family Member
Is Using Porn

Husbands, love your wives, just as Christ loved the church and gave himself up for her. (Eph 5:25)

I have had phone calls from friends who reveal to me how porn has damaged their marriages. These good people not only go to church but are actively engaged at their churches. I have talked to parents who have discovered that their innocent young children have been looking at porn for years already, becoming addicted even before puberty. I have heard of countless marriages that have been ripped apart because of pornography. I have also seen dating relationships ruined, kids feeling isolated from their parents, young adults isolated from their family due to shame, and much more.

Porn ruins lives. Porn destroys relationships. Porn kills love. But it can't kill hope. Jesus always brings us hope and a chance at redemption, healing, and forgiveness. Jesus binds up the wounds that drive people apart.

A parent, wife, husband, or other family member often feels helpless when someone in the home is using pornography. They may feel guilt, suspicion, or betrayal, or that they are being used or are not good enough. Many other negative issues also need to be dealt with. Too often porn is seen as a personal issue, but the pain and suffering it causes affect many others. These relationships and individuals need healing, as do those who are using porn.

Children Using Porn

If you are a parent, do you know if your twelve-year-old has ever seen pornography? If you don't know, he or she probably has. Too many young people have been exposed to porn. This means we are raising a generation of hyper-sexualized children who don't fully understand what is happening to them. Their brains aren't close to full development, which happens in young adulthood, and they usually don't know what sex is all about. In other words, porn is training kids to be lifelong sex addicts.

I don't know any parents who want their preteen child to be a sex addict. I know you don't want that for your child, but to avoid it in our culture, you must be vigilant and proactive. You should not wait until a problem develops. If your child does have a problem, you can't just believe it will go away on its own.

If you have found your child looking at porn, the first thing you should do is examine your own reaction to this discovery. How do you feel? Disappointed? Sad? Scared? Angry? These are natural reactions. But you don't necessarily want to let your child know this. You ought to let your kid know he or she has done something wrong, but you still need to show love for your child. More than anything, you should demonstrate concern for his or her well-being. It's as if you have discovered that your child has a life-threatening disease and you have the cure, but it will take the next few years to administer. It will mean suffering and setbacks, but you can do it.

The first step is to let you child know that you love him or her. Always make sure to stress that your love is not conditional. You will also have to reassert strict boundaries. If this means backtracking on privileges, such as having a phone, access to friends, dating someone, spending time alone, getting on electronic media, or similar situations, you must follow through with it.

If your child is open to working on the problem with you, things will not be as difficult as they would be if the child opposed you. Some children will resist every effort a parent makes, because they haven't seen using porn for the problem it is. It might take much education, outside help, and strict boundaries to help them start to build the desire to stop. Understand that you have broken down the barrier of privacy and silence. Therefore, your son or daughter may experience great shame, defensiveness, anger, withdrawal from the family, and sadness. You must respond with compassion and gentleness, even if they lash out at you.

Let your child know that their confidences won't be broken unless necessary. You might explain that you will keep their secret as long as doing so does not endanger your child or another person. (Mental health professionals who work with your child will always need to know.) You might even give some options for how they might seek help, within reason. For instance, you might let them choose between two counselors— a man and a woman. But don't let them choose whether or not to get professional help, if needed. Even if your child actively works against your attempts to help, don't give up. Your children need you now more than ever. Love them with all you have and never stop working to help your child with this problem.

Spouse Using Porn

More and more women are using pornography. A wife who uses pornography is not as rare as before, though men still use porn at a higher rate than women. Still, whether it is a wife or a husband, a spouse using porn will hurt you, your children, and your marriage, as well as himself or herself. All of these hurts must be acknowledged so healing may take place for all of them.

When a spouse discovers his or her partner is using porn regularly, many emotions may be strongly felt: anger, discouragement, sadness, resentment, and more. The issue can be magnified if the spouse using porn tries to justify it, rationalize it, or make the other person feel responsible.

Many spouses who use porn struggle to understand the turmoil and desolation their spouses feel. They may never intend to hurt their wife or husband, but if they are callous to the destructive nature of their acts, it can compound the hurt. It is absolutely necessary for the spouse using porn to acknowledge that he or she is responsible and has wounded the other person.

Wendy and Larry Maltz have identified four stages in a relationship marked by porn:[1]

STAGE 1: **Being in the dark**. In this stage one spouse uses porn but the other spouse doesn't know about it. Damage can occur in this stage because problems in the relationship are not yet acknowledged. The partners are not yet discussing the issue of porn.

Porn isn't just a teenage or young adult problem. It can impact people of almost any age. Some or even many people you know struggle with this problem. The same goes for many spouses—they may not know their partner is an addict, but it affects them nonetheless.

STAGE 2: **The shock of discovery**. Imagine being the spouse of someone who hid a porn problem for many years. Now imagine the intense hurt when he or she finally reveals it to you. Many readers of this book have experienced that unimaginable hurt. Some have accidentally discovered their spouses using porn. Some have suspected it and found the evidence when they looked for it. Other spouses finally admitted their problem on their own. No matter how one finds out, the revelation will be crushing.

Even if one spouse is in the dark about the other's problem, porn will cause sexual, emotional, and other difficulties in a marriage. These will only grow as porn use increases. The other

---

1. Wendy Maltz and Larry Maltz, *The Porn Trap: The Essential Guide to Overcoming Problems Caused by Pornography* (New York: Harper, 2008), 96–119.

spouse may wonder what is causing the problems. He or she may ask: "Did I do something wrong? Why am I not good enough? Does my spouse still love me?"

The porn user, instead, may think that using porn isn't an issue, or may rationalize that everyone uses it. This is especially true when the husband uses porn and his wife is in the dark. Men will rationalize their use of porn as a way to fulfill their "greater" desire for sex. Some will say they didn't think it would hurt their wives. Still more think it isn't a big deal. All of these excuses are lies and ways of keeping the issue hidden. Yet the problem will cause stress, anxiety, and relationship problems in every case.

Every person who discovers that his or her spouse is using porn will feel betrayed. Some may become embittered and many seek divorce, believing the relationship can never be healed. The pain cannot be overstated.

STAGE 3: **Emotional wounds.** Even after the yelling, crying, and emotional outbursts have started to calm down, the hurt still exists. Deep emotional wounds should be acknowledged by both spouses. Many will feel insecure and lonely. Some will resist having sex with their spouse. Others may even start to distance themselves from their spouse, while still others have a lowered sense of self-esteem, believing they are part of the problem.

The porn user may believe the expression of pain is over-blown or has gone on too long. I have heard from many spouses who wish they had never started looking at porn, because they didn't think it could cause such pain in others. Trust has been shattered and may never be the same again. The wounds from porn use do not differ much from the wounds of a real-life affair.

The difficulties can continue to grow even if a porn user tries to stop. It only takes one more instance of porn use for the pain to start all over again. The relationship may never go back to being as it was, but things can get better if healing is accepted by both spouses.

STAGE 4: **Trying to cope.** Some spouses may try to "fix" the porn user. They may become vigilant in tracking their spouse's every move. They might even try to compete with the porn sexually. None of these strategies will help; only seeking out and accepting the help of others can truly assist in healing. This help can come through a wise counselor, a small group, a prudent spiritual guide, a twelve-step support group, or a combination of these.

Activities and Questions

1. Do you have a family member who is using porn? If so, in what ways has this affected you? How do you feel about it?

2. You will need healing and help. How do you plan to seek this out?

3. What could you do to help others who are using porn? Write down at least three ideas.

CHAPTER 9

How to Talk to Your Kids about Sex

Train children in the right way, and when old, they will not stray. (Prov 22:6)

I am blessed to speak to many audiences around the country. In two of my presentations at a homeschooling conference, I briefly mentioned the dangers of pornography and the need for parents to talk to their children about sexuality. After the talks, I was flooded with questions from parents wanting to know how they should talk to their children.

One thing I told them, as I stated earlier, is that responding to their children's questions merely with a no is not enough. The no to sex outside of marriage between one man and one woman can still be a small part of the conversation, but should never be the heart of it.

We have to give our kids something to say yes to. Children can say no to pornography and illicit sex only when they have a bigger yes they can respond to positively. God is much bigger than pleasure or sex. Love sometimes means delaying gratification, limiting yourself, and being ready to sacrifice. Marriages are strengthened by people who have such virtue and self-control. In fact, you can't give away what you don't control. If you want to give yourself away to the one you are married to, then you must first have self-control.

Furthermore, parents need to talk with their kids about the big picture of relationships. The following questions could be some useful ways to start a discussion:

➤ Why do people date and marry? Because we are made for relationships and loving others can draw us all closer to God and heaven.

➤ Why do we have these desires and feelings? They come from God and point to our need for him.

➤ Is it okay to have these desires and feelings? Of course.

➤ How do we properly channel them? By learning chastity and self-control.

➤ What does appropriate intimacy look like (whether emotionally or physically)? It depends on the level of the relationship, but true intimacy should be reserved for marriage.

These questions and many more come up when you talk to your kids about sex and relationships.

Why You Must Talk to Your Kids about Sex!

If *you* don't teach them, someone else will. Schools, friends, and the wider culture (TV, movies, music) are already shoving a false image of sex down your kids' throats. You need to have the loudest and clearest voice in this conversation. Now is the time to educate your kids proactively, not reactively. The Catholic Church has always taught that parents are the primary educators of their children. To teach our kids is an obligation and a gift! You need to educate yourself so you can properly educate your children. Reading this book is merely the first step. You can't give what you don't have, and your kids can't love the truth if they don't know it.

Even if some conversations are uncomfortable, having them with your children can only help them and the rest of your family. Just make sure you talk to them about many topics, not only about sex and porn. Talking about important subjects teaches your kids communication within the family. Regular communication about the problems, emotions, joys, and struggles of life can be the foundation of a strong relationship with your child(ren).

Moreover, our job as parents is not only to protect our children from things that may harm them. Rather, we should prepare them to change the culture they live in for themselves, future generations, the common good, and the glory of God. Thus, the goal of talking to your kids about sex is not to put a virtual chastity belt on your kids, but to prepare them for what they will face in life.

Remember—talking to your kids about sex isn't about you! You don't need to discuss your own sexual baggage, nor should it keep you from talking to your kids about sex. Your job as a parent is to form, teach, model, and help your children. Ultimately, they will make their own decisions and sometimes mess up. Your goal isn't to control your children's lives forever, but to set them on a course for success in life. Formation with your children is like a tunnel. At the back of the tunnel, when your children are small, they need tight boundaries, so they are given little freedom. This is necessary to protect them. The older they get the wider the passage gets, and they will have fewer boundaries. Once they leave your house they have no boundaries outside of themselves, set by your rules. If you have formed them well, they will have interior boundaries that will help protect them.

One of the goals my wife and I have set as parents is to guide our children up to the point of their senior year in high school. During the final year each of our kids will spend in our house, they will have to take care of all their own responsibilities, just as they will in college, but under our watch. Thus, they will have to wake themselves, pay their bills, make sure their homework is done, do their own laundry, and so forth for one year, as my wife and I guide them gently toward adulthood. While this kind of parenting is contrary to the modern idea of the helicopter parent (one who constantly monitors all activities and is always there to save the child from harm), it appears to us to be more prudent.

Your kids want you to help them. Even if they will never admit it, the most important people in their lives are their parents. So when your kid initiates a conversation about sex, relationships, or any other important topic, drop everything else and focus on that, spending whatever time you need to listen. Try not to overreact if your kid has something shocking to tell you. If a parent overreacts to a mistake or a confession of an issue a child brings to Mom or Dad, it may keep the child from reaching out to you again.

True, the culture could destroy your kid's life. You should talk about the negative realities of having sex with someone you aren't married to, even if you don't focus only on that. Sometimes people need a negative reason to say no. Single mothers, STDs, broken hearts, failed marriages, and other ills are all reasons not to have extramarital sex, even if they aren't the best reasons. Natural consequences happen. Kids know this.

Your children's souls are worth whatever discomfort you may feel when talking to your kids! Don't forget the spiritual reality that sexual sin can kill the supernatural grace of God in a person. Remember also the two levels of forgiveness—fear and love. The lower is fear of punishment, but it is enough to have your sins forgiven. The higher is love of God. If it takes fear to get someone to do the right thing, use it. But use it appropriately— hellfire and brimstone notwithstanding.

How to Talk to Your Kids and What to Talk About

Focus on what is most important. While you need to talk about biology, the conversations you have with your kids should focus on God's plan for our lives, character, virtue, morality, and relationships. Don't just talk about the biological facts and the anatomy of boys and girls.

Teach them the big picture of sex, using the Church's teachings on sexuality and love, especially the theology of the body (see next chapter). God made us sexual beings for a reason.

Healthy humans are persons who have integrated their sexuality. We need to teach our kids how to do this.

Our bodies are a reflection of God. We are made in God's image and likeness, and this includes our bodies, not merely our souls. Our bodies can be used for great good (imaging God, worship, love) or great evil. They are temples of the Holy Spirit made for good.

If needed, use good resources. (See the resources section at the end of this book.) Go through materials with your child rather than just giving them things to use on their own. You needn't feel tethered to any particular resources. Add to or take out whatever you think is best.

Even if the conversation feels awkward, be comfortable with your own limitations. Do your best and give your child what you have. Nobody else can take your place in this conversation.

Teach your kids what love really is. Remember, true love equals choosing what is best for another, despite what it might cost. This kind of love is not easy, but it certainly is worth it. Though it takes sacrifice and effort, it is the kind of love we are created by and for. This kind of love says yes to loving another person by not having sex until marriage.

As the Church has always taught, sex has a dual purpose—babies and bonding (the unitive and procreative purposes of sex). Talk about both. Remember that this should never be a one-time conversation, but an ongoing series. Make this formation a part of your family.

The conversations need to start at a young age. How young? Seven to eight years old is a good starting point, because many children will start to be exposed to porn in late elementary school and junior high. You have to talk to them before the culture gets them.

If possible, start the conversation with both parents present. Mom and Dad and child is the optimal formula, especially at early ages. In many situations (single-parent homes, military families, one parent's lack of interest, among others) it may not be possible for both parents to participate. Don't let being alone stop you from having these important conversations.

Try to communicate with one kid at a time, to stress the subject's importance. As the children get older, dads should talk to sons about male issues if possible, and moms should talk to their daughters. This is especially helpful when talking about puberty. Naturally occurring conversations with the entire family are okay, as long as you take younger children into consideration.

Of course we will never parent perfectly, so through all the mistakes, bad decisions, and errors we make, we can still do a good job of loving our kids and setting them up for success—if we do our best starting now. All parents also continue to learn and grow in how they parent, so please seek out other parents who might walk with you on this journey and from whom you can seek advice. No matter what, resolve to do the best you can—for your children's sake as well as your own.

Activities and Questions

1. If you have already talked to your child(ren) about sex, what did you talk about and what did you avoid?

2. What resources, if any, do you use to talk to your child(ren) about sex? Have they helped you? If so, in what ways?

3. What are some other ways that your child(ren) might learn about sex? How can you talk about these with your child(ren)?

CHAPTER 10

The Catholic Antidote to Porn

Therefore a man leaves his father and his mother and clings to his wife, and they become one flesh. And the man and his wife were both naked, and were not ashamed. (Gen 2:24–25)

What is the Catholic antidote to porn? It is found in Jesus and it has several steps:

1. Knowing who we truly are and rejecting the lies about ourselves.

2. Knowing the truth about what we are created for.

3. Living out the purpose of our lives, given to us by God.

4. Making the right decisions, even when they are difficult to make.

5. Turning to God in our times of need.

6. Saying yes to something better than porn.

Who Are You?

What kind of person do you want to be? Do you want to be kind or mean? Do you want to be brave or cowardly? Do you want to be honest or dishonest? Do you want to be faithful or unfaithful? Do you want to be addicted to porn or free from it? Do you want good relationships with others?

The answers to these questions might surprise you, because many of us have mixed feelings about them. Some of us want it both ways, but that isn't possible. We must choose what kind of person we want to be and acknowledge who we currently are.

We humans have lost our identity, having forgotten we are made in God's image. But we still face the big questions: Who am I? What is life's purpose? Who is God? Why was I created?

These questions and the corresponding answers directly influence what we believe, how we view life, and how we live. Here is the root of the issue: without an identity in Christ, we cannot see ourselves, others, or the world in the proper context. We mistake a lie for the truth.

What is the truth about our identity in Jesus? It is that each of us is created in the image and likeness of God. Big deal, you might think. But it is. It is our identity. We are adopted into the family of God (the Trinity) by our Baptism, and thus we share in the divine nature. This means our own human nature is caught up into God and participates in God's divine life. A new-found identity in Jesus means we can no longer look at ourselves or others in the same way.

Of course, this relationship with God can also be lost if we choose to commit mortal sin and cut God out of our lives. Still, this divine life, which is infused in our souls by God's grace, is a great gift that can lead us to understand the depth of our own dignity. This is why Saint John Paul the Great quoted the following line from the Vatican II document *Gauduim et Spes* more than any other: "Christ, the final Adam, by the revelation of the mystery of the Father and his love, fully reveals man to man himself and makes his supreme calling clear."[1]

If we want to know who we are, who others are, and the answers to the other questions that have been planted deep within us, we need to understand who Jesus is and who we are in the light of Christ. When God became man in the incarnation, he didn't lower his own divine nature, which is impossible because God is unchangeable; rather he lifted up our human nature. "For by his incarnation the Son of God has united himself in some fashion with every man."[2]

This is our supreme calling: to find who we are in Christ, and to live fully in the Father's love, truth, and grace. God made us for this. Here we find the truth about the mystery of humanity. We were made to live this way, to find this truth. When we do so, we find what real human dignity means. "Only in the mystery of Jesus, God made man, does the mystery of what it means to be human take on light."[3]

---

1. *Pastoral Constitution on the Church in the Modern World* — Gaudium et Spes. Promulgated by Pope Paul VI. (Vatican City: 1965), http://www.vatican.va/archive/hist_councils/ii_vatican_council/documents/vat-ii_const_19651207_gaudium-et-spes_en.html

2. Ibid.

3. Ibid.

When we do not live in this truth we bring suffering upon ourselves and others. This is the root of *every* problem in our society today. Let me offer a few examples.

1. **Abortion.** When we do not see a developing baby in light of the mystery of God and humanity, then the dignity of a baby, who can't act as we act, is lost. Babies become something that impedes our attempt to be happy, as we understand it. They inconvenience us.

   But if we see babies through the eternal eyes of God, they have an inestimable value. They are priceless, and their dignity does not depend on what they "do." Their identity is being a son or daughter of the Father. They are the brothers and sisters of the God-Man, Jesus.

2. **The poor.** How would I treat my own children if they came to me hungry and asked for food? I would give it them. Just so, when God's children are in need, we are called to treat them as God's children, not as an inconvenience. If we see them as the persons they truly are, we can only do what is best for them within our means.

3. **Self-esteem/self-worth.** Whenever we see ourselves as worthless or without dignity, we fail to see ourselves in light of the incarnation. God took on flesh, not for his own sake, but for my sake and yours. He became a man in order to show that nothing is more worthy of love than the height of his visible creation: human beings. Nothing is more worthy of love than you. This love is not merely a feeling, but a sacrificial love. Through this love, Jesus humbled himself to live and die for another. That is love. It is for you.

4. **Suffering**. Without Jesus crucified, suffering has no purpose. It is to be avoided at all costs, the worst thing that can happen to us. Without the crucifix, pleasure becomes the highest good. But pleasure comes and goes. When it is gone, our lives lose meaning. The cross rightly orders our lives. It points us to the real meaning of life: living in the truth of who we are as humans made by God for sacrificial love. In this identity we can discover why God allows suffering: to draw us closer to himself.

5. **Relationships**. When we enter a relationship with another person who is as valuable as we are, we will do nothing but truly love the other person, giving wholly of ourselves. We will never treat another as someone who exists for us, but rather who exists for God. Other persons are never to be used. They are always to be valued. What we say to them and what we do with them will always reflect this reality. More than anything, we must never use God's own beloved for our selfish pleasure or expose them to danger, whether physical, mental, spiritual, or social. Chastity and charity are the virtues that spring from such a relationship.

These few examples show how the theology of the body is a big part of the antidote to the problems in our culture.

The Theology of the Body

I have heard this accusation many times: the Catholic Church is hung up on sex and needs to take care of its own house before telling us what to do! This accusation reflects a strategy of deflect and accuse. Deflect blame for the culture's over-sexualization and remind others of problems to avoid dealing with the real issue. Our culture is saturated in sex. I don't even need to offer examples, because we see this reality every day.

In a culture such as this, how can we respond? What is it that can help us recapture a true vision of sex that many have lost, including most Catholics? It begins by understanding what happened in the "beginning."

When John Paul II became pope, he brought with him a rich background in understanding human relationships, especially marriage and sexual love between husband and wife. As a pastor, he had frequently met with parishioners and married friends. He had a great deal of practical knowledge in addition to the philosophy and theology he had studied. Ultimately, his reflections on humanity, relationships, love, and God led him to teach and write about these subjects in an enlightened way. What we have received from him can be called a "theology of the body," and it contains good news for us.

All theology tells us something about God; John Paul II's insight is called a theology of the body because our bodies tell us about God. Because we are made in the image and likeness of God, and because our bodies are part of who we are, our bodies reflect something about God in a way that no other part of creation does.

In this theology, John Paul II teaches that sex is not just a bodily function or an emotional reaction. Rather, sexual union is a human act. If we have the eyes to see the truth about our sexuality, this truth can change our lives so that sexuality becomes a great gift to us, not a problem or something that rules over us.

The gift doesn't come without difficulties, however. Many people have struggled to understand John Paul II's philosophical language and style. He was a very intelligent and insightful man, but he wrote in a way that can be difficult for the average Catholic to understand.

Furthermore, John Paul II had what might be best described as a corkscrew method to his thinking. In other words, he would return to the same topic again and again, but he would approach it from a different viewpoint. He did this to find new insights into what he had already taught, still building on his teaching. Neither of the issues with John Paul II's writing style—his corkscrew method and his dense philosophical language—allows for an easy read. Therefore, many people who have tried to read his teaching on human sexuality have given up in frustration.

Still, I believe the attempt to mine the theology of the body from John Paul II can bear much fruit. In fact, it has transformed my own life. When I started to study his teachings on humanity, God, sexuality, our purpose in life, and how they are all interconnected, I was blown away. Its profound impact sparked a huge conversion in my own life, second only to my initial conversion, when I first decided to follow Jesus.[4] I believe John Paul II's teaching on the theology of the body can be an opportunity for conversion for you as well, even if you are struggling with your sexuality or addicted to porn.

---

4. Marcel LeJeune, *Set Free to Love: Lives Changed by the Theology of the Body* (Cincinnati: Servant, 2010).

The Beginning of Everything

John Paul II (born Karol Wojtyła) suffered a great deal in his life, starting from a young age. Both his mother and brother died before Karol was an adult, and his only sister died before he was born. So he lived alone with his father for much of his youth. His father, a devout man of prayer, guided his son through war, suffering, and strife. Karol was a talented actor, a devoted athlete, and a man who learned at a young age how to dive deep into prayer.

Through practicing prayer, Karol started to discern a call to the priesthood. But this desire soon met a big obstacle. World War II broke out when the Nazis invaded his native Poland. Still he persevered. Continuing his studies in a clandestine seminary, Karol became keenly aware of how God could ultimately bring good from any evil situation.

As Karol pondered the evil in the world, he responded by juxtaposing the lies around him (including communism, fascism, utilitarianism, and nihilism) with the truth taught by Jesus Christ. This truth included the profound mystery of God and his amazingly desperate pursuit of humanity, which ends with Jesus becoming one of us and raising our human dignity to a new level. The common thread among the false worldviews and philosophies that Karol started to counter was that they all failed to see the amazing worth of each human being—and God himself as the source of that worth.

When Karol became a priest, he began to minister to young people, many of them married. He heard their confessions, counseled them, and became their friend. He pondered in prayer and then wrote down his personal reflections, applying his philosophical studies in a practical way. This was the origin of his theology of the body. He intended to publish these reflections in one volume, but before he could do that he was elected pope. From 1979 to 1984 he delivered these teachings in a new format, in his Wednesday general audiences to the Church.

Ultimately, the theology of the body is based upon a deep examination of several different parts of the Bible. The first is the creation account of man and woman in the Book of Genesis. In his reflections, John Paul II speaks about what life was like for Adam and Eve before, during, and after the fall from grace. He also reflects on how sin terribly impacted the purpose of their relationship and the depth of their identity. Through these teachings, he gave us deep insights into the Christian understanding of humanity (an anthropology), as well as insights into how our very bodies reflect God (a theology).

Created with Meaning

Most people, even many non-Christians, believe they know the story of Adam and Eve. But John Paul II broke open their story in a way many people have never heard before. Adam, being the ideal man (because he had no sin), was created in a close relationship with his Creator due to the gift of grace. He communed with God. John Paul II called this relationship between God and Adam "original solitude." Even though it appears God has given Adam everything he could ever need, Adam still longs for something more.

God states, "It is not good that the man should be alone" (Gen 2:18). Then he puts Adam into a deep sleep in order to create Eve. Though created in a perfect relationship with God, Adam was created with another need—for a relationship with another human. This is the one thing God could not provide by himself for Adam—a helper who was like Adam in dignity, but still different in other ways. All of us have this longing, and what God sees in Adam is what he sees in each of us. We have a need for a helpmate who can love us (reciprocated by us) in a communion of persons—a relationship of equals. Adam finds his helpmate in Eve. Thus, the first human relationship is the one between husband and wife. Through this relationship, we find the origin of all other human relationships. The communion between a husband and wife cannot be undervalued, especially in a culture that does not understand the primordial importance of this most basic human relationship.

At this point in the story, Adam and Eve are completely naked, but they have no lust. It is hard for us to understand how that could be, and its even more difficult if we struggle with porn. Many of you may ask how Adam or Eve could look on each other and not lust? How could they not want to use each other for pleasure? How is this possible? In the state of original innocence Adam and Eve possessed before sin entered the garden, neither had any desire to use the other person. Once they sinned, they lost this grace and fell into a state of concupiscence, that is, they now had the natural tendency to sin, which we have all inherited. Still, John Paul II provides an even deeper answer for us.

The mysterious relationship between humanity and God is given a deeper meaning in Jesus (who is both God and man). John Paul II teaches that our human bodies reflect something about God. This is one aspect of how we are made in God's image and likeness. This enables us to reflect back to the world something about God himself. What is it we reflect? One insight is that the bodies of both men and women are made to come together in a communion of persons. Before we ever enter into a sexual relationship in marriage, we are all called into other kinds of relationships. Even once we enter into the covenantal relationship within marriage, this communion of persons precedes the sexual bonding that furthers the relationship.

Still, sex helps give our bodies meaning! This is a profound statement for someone who is struggling with sexuality, but it can help us understand the value of our sexuality. Our sexuality is made to be ordered toward the good of the other person, not merely our sexual arousal and pleasure. Once we have properly ordered our sexuality, it can be a natural outgrowth of how we love our spouses and reflect God's goodness. One of the more profound statements of John Paul II is that "the body, and it alone, is capable of making visible what is invisible."[5]

Our bodies are capable of making the life of the Trinity known to us. This is because male and female bodies have a deep meaning built within them. They each reflect God's goodness in and of themselves, but without the other, we are not able to completely show several aspects of the nature of God. We are made for one another. We are even made to have sex and, in the sexual act, we do two things we can't do alone: create new life and reflect the Trinity in a new way. We image the Trinity because there is a true complementarity in man and woman having married, sexual love. This is because the Trinity has everything needed to form a family: one who loves another (the Father), one who is loved (the Son), and the love between them

---

5. John Paul II, General Audience of Wednesday, Feb. 20, 1980, https://w2.vatican.va/content/john-paul-ii/en/audiences/1980/documents/hf_jp-ii_aud_19800220.html.

(the Holy Spirit). Because the Holy Spirit is the love between the Father and the Son, Scripture says, "God is love" (1 Jn 4:8). A man and his wife can reflect this Trinitarian love when they have sex and procreate children who then reflect the love between the parents.

Once I discovered what my sexuality was truly meant for, it changed my life and my marriage. I now understand the depth of meaning God has instilled in each one of us. God loves us desperately. He loves us so much that he endowed every part of our being with great meaning, both in our souls and in our bodies. This meaning resides in every fiber of our being, even those places where we might find it hard to find God—our sexuality.

Redemption

Love is about much more than sex. This truth is sometimes minimized by an over-sexualized culture, but can never be truly hidden. We all need love and are made to live in love, to love others, to love God, and to allow ourselves to be loved back. Yet none of us loves perfectly in this life, because we all suffer from Adam and Eve's fall from grace. We are no longer in the Garden of Eden; we have all sinned.

When sin entered the world, lust came with it. This is why Adam and Eve quickly made clothes out of fig leaves. They hid their bodies from the lustful eyes of the other. Their shame is a natural reaction to the lust of someone else; in fact, it is a defensive posture we all must have as long as lust is in the world. Lust is the desire to use another person for a selfish purpose. Ultimately, using another person is the opposite of real love, according to John Paul II.

Still, we aren't made to stay in this sinful state, but to fight sin with virtue, which is strengthened by God's grace. After the Fall, humanity needs grace. We cannot recapture our dignity by ourselves. But God doesn't abandon us; he sent us his Son, Jesus, to rescue us from sin and death.

By Jesus becoming a man, suffering, dying, and rising again, he has conquered sin and death and allowed us the opportunity to go to heaven. All the graces we ever need to go to heaven have been won by Jesus, but now we must participate in our own redemption by saying yes to Jesus and unlocking the power of those graces in our lives.

Doing this isn't easy. Each of us has absorbed many lies about ourselves, and the healing won't be easy. Yet we are made for this journey! The theology of the body stands as a paradox to the modern ideas of sex and the body. It communicates a new path for us, a path of freedom, holiness, and purity. It calls us to love and virtue. It gives us a vision for life that doesn't reject sex or lift it up as the greatest good. Rather, it rightly teaches us the holy purpose of our bodies.

Mystery

If you are married you are given the responsibility of loving and caring for one of God's sons or daughters in your spouse. If you are a parent, you are given care over God's children in your own offspring. All of us are given care over the greatest thing God has ever created: the people we have relationships with. We cannot overstate the worth of each human person, even those who are part of pornographic depictions of sex or those who consume porn. Each life has value. Each person reflects God's love. Each of us has a sexuality that is meant to reflect God. Sex has a sacred value, and we are called to something much better than degrading it with porn.

My prayer for each of you is that you will know and live out this immense value that has been stamped into your very bodies and the bodies of others. May we all grow closer to God and one another while learning that porn is never the answer. When we say yes to the beauty of God's plan, which is so much better than the ugliness of porn, we will find the happiness Jesus promised to the pure of heart.

Activities and Questions

1. Who are you and why are you worth so much to God?

2. Why did God give you your sexuality? What is the purpose of sex?

3. What misunderstandings of your nature and sexuality have you mistakenly held?

4. Write a letter from God to someone you love. Allow our Heavenly Father to give voice to how much he loves this person, through you. Now cross out the name and put your own. Put it in an envelope and address it to yourself. Ask your accountability partner to hang on to the letter and mail it sometime in the future.

---------- APPENDIX 1 ----------

Resources

BOOKS

Help with the Problem of Porn

Be Healed: A Guide to Encountering the Powerful Love of Jesus in Your Life by Bob Schuchts. Notre Dame, IN: Ave Maria Press, 2014.

Integrity Restored: Helping Catholic Families Win the Battle Against Pornography by Peter C. Kleponis. Steubenville, OH: Emmaus Road Publishing, 2014.

Overcoming Pornography Addiction: A Spiritual Solution by J. Brian Bransfield. Mahwah, NJ: Paulist Press, 2013.

Fortify: A Step Toward Recovery by Fight The New Drug. Salt Lake City, UT: O.W.L. Publishing, 2013.

Healing the Wounds of Sexual Addiction by Mark R. Laaser. Grand Rapids, MI: Zondervan, 2004.

The Pornography Trap: A Resource for Ministry Leaders by Mark Laaser and Ralph Earle. Kansas City, MO: Beacon Hill Press, 2012.

For Parents

Beyond the Birds and the Bees: Raising Sexually Whole and Holy Kids by Gregory K. Popcak and Lisa Popcak. West Chester, PA: Ascension Press, 2012.

Facing the Facts: The Truth About Sex and You: God's Design for Sex by Stanton L. Jones and Brenna B. Jones. Colorado Springs, CO: NavPress, 2007.

Good Pictures Bad Pictures: Porn-Proofing Today's Young Kids by Kristen A. Jenson. Richland, WA: Glen Cove Press, 2015.

Raising Pure Teens: 10 Strategies to Protect or Restore Your Teenager's Innocence by Jason Evert and Chris Stefanick. San Diego, CA: Catholic Answers, 2010.

Sex, Love & You: Making the Right Decision by Tom and Judy Lickona, with William Boudreau. Notre Dame, IN: Ave Maria Press, 2003.

What's the Big Deal? Why God Cares About Sex (God's Design for Sex) by Stanton L. Jones and Brenna B. Jones. Colorado Springs, CO: NavPress, 2007.

For Teens and Young Adults

God's Plan For You: Life, Love, Marriage, and Sex by David Hajduk. Boston, MA: Pauline Books & Media, 2006.

If You Really Loved Me: 100 Questions on Dating, Relationships, and Sexual Purity by Jason Evert. Cincinnati, OH: Servant Books, 2009.

Pure Manhood by Jason Evert. San Diego, CA: Catholic Answers Press, 2007.

Pure Womanhood by Crystalina Evert. San Diego, CA: Catholic Answers Press, 2012.

Theology of the Body for Teens: Discovering God's Plan for Love and Life by Brian Butler, Jason Evert, Colin MacIver, and Aimee MacIver. Westchester, PA: Ascension Press, 2011.

What's the Big Deal About Pornography? A Guide for the Internet Generation by Jill C. Manning. Salt Lake City, UT: Shadow Mountain, 2008.

Testimonies of Freedom from Sexual Problems

Delivered: True Stories of Men and Women Who Turned from Porn to Purity by Matt Fradd. San Diego, CA: Catholic Answers Press, 2014.

Not Ready for Marriage, Not Ready for Sex: One Couple's Return to Chastity by Chris Padgett and Linda Padgett. Cincinnati, OH: Servant Books, 2006.

Set Free to Love: Lives Changed by the Theology of the Body by Marcel LeJeune. Cincinnati, OH: Servant Books, 2010.

Understanding Catholic Teaching on Sexuality

Adam and Eve after the Pill: Paradoxes of the Sexual Revolution by Mary Eberstadt. San Francisco, CA: Ignatius Press, 2013.

Catholicism and Contraception: What the Church Teaches and Why by Angela Franks. Boston, MA: Pauline Books & Media, 2013.

Good News About Sex & Marriage: Answers to Your Honest Questions about Catholic Teaching by Christopher West. Cincinnati, OH: Servant Books, 2004.

Men, Women, and the Mystery of Love: Practical Insights from John Paul II's Love and Responsibility by Edward Sri. Cincinnati, OH: Servant Books, 2007.

Man and Woman He Created Them: A Theology of the Body by Pope John Paul II, translated and with an introduction by Michael Waldstein. Boston, MA: Pauline Books & Media, 2006.

Theology of the Body for Beginners: A Basic Introduction to Pope John Paul II's Sexual Revolution by Christopher West. Westchester, PA: Ascension Press, 2009.

Theology of the Body Made Simple by Anthony Percy. Boston, MA: Pauline Books & Media, 2006.

Spouses of Addicts

Deceived: Facing Sexual Betrayal, Lies, and Secrets by Claudia Black. Center City, MN: Hazelden, 2009.

Facing Heartbreak: Steps to Recovery for Partners of Sex Addicts by Stefanie Carnes, Mari A. Lee, and Anthony Rodriguez. Carefree, AZ: Gentle Path Press, 2012.

Hope After Betrayal: Healing When Sexual Addiction Invades Your Marriage by Meg Wilson. Grand Rapids, MI: Kregel Publications, 2007.

Mending a Shattered Heart: A Guide for Partners of Sex Addicts by Stefanie Carnes. Carefree, AZ: Gentle Path Press, 2011.

Shattered Vows: Hope and Healing for Women Who Have Been Sexually Betrayed by Debra Laaser. Grand Rapids, MI: Zondervan, 2008.

The Science of Porn Addiction

Facing the Shadow: Starting Sexual and Relationship Recovery by Patrick J. Carnes. Carefree, AZ: Gentle Path Press, 2008.

Out of the Shadows: Understanding Sexual Addiction by Patrick J. Carnes. Center City, MN: Hazelden, 2001.

The Porn Trap: The Essential Guide to Overcoming Problems Caused by Pornography by Wendy Maltz and Larry Maltz. New York: Harper Collins, 2010.

Shadows of the Cross: A Christian Companion to Facing the Shadow by Craig S. Cashwell, Pennie K. Johnson, and Patrick J. Carnes. Carefree, AZ: Gentle Path Press, 2015.

Wired for Intimacy: How Pornography Hijacks the Male Brain by William M. Struthers. Downers Grove, IL: IVP Books, 2009.

WEB SITES

Media/Internet Filters

www.covenanteyes.com

www.opendns.com

www.netnanny.com

www1.k9webprotection.com

Web site Resources

endsexualexploitation.org (National Center on Sexual Exploitation)

www.socialcostsofpornography.com

thetheologyofthebody.com

www.tobinstitute.org (Theology of the Body Institute)

Help with Porn

chastityproject.com

pornproofkids.org

chastity.com

fightthenewdrug.org

theporneffect.com

thekingsmen.us

integrityrestored.com

reclaimsexualhealth.com

www.sa.org

couragerc.org

jpiihealingcenter.org

markchamberlainphd.blogspot.com

Format and Principles for Accountability Groups

I have been running accountability groups for men for the past twelve years. Below is the basic format and the principles I use. The groups meet weekly for prayer, learning, discussion, and to help the men support and encourage one another. The groups are generally limited to twelve members or fewer, because the group loses its intimacy once they get larger. The format below is not the only way to run an accountability group, but includes many of the basics that other groups use as well.

Format

STEP 1: **Before the group—a basic interview.**

Once a young man contacts me, I meet with him one on one before allowing him to be a part of the group. The purpose is to gauge where he is coming from and what he has experienced, and to see if the group might help him. I ask several questions, including the following:

> ➤ At what age did the problem start?

> ➤ How often do you look at porn and masturbate?

> ➤ Have you tried to stop? What is the longest you have gone without acting out?

> ➤ Do you have any same-sex attractions?

> ➤ Do you currently have a sexual relationship with anyone?

> ➤ What do you hope to get out of the group?

I also warn him up front that I will be required by law to report any abuse of minors or use of child pornography. I am very honest; I tell him the group is not a quick fix and that it will take many difficult day-to-day decisions in order to change. I then tell him what goes on when the group meets. Everything is completely confidential; we don't tell anyone where or when we meet. We don't disclose who is in the group or what anyone says there. I also ask whether he is willing to abide by these rules. If he agrees, he must sign a covenant form.

Finally, I ask if there are any questions. If I think the group might help him, I ask if he believes he is ready to join and commit to the group. Only if he agrees do I tell him when and where we meet.

Step 2: *Group principles.*

During the first meeting of the accountability group, we start with a reminder about the group's principles. They include:

1. We observe strict confidentiality about content, participants, time, location, and so on.

2. We share only what we feel called to share. We always trust that we are in a safe place. We encourage everyone to share; otherwise the group will not benefit the individual or other participants.

3. Even if we have to challenge a brother to step up and do better, we never shame him or make him feel unworthy. We always practice gentleness and kindness, yet we are called to hold one another accountable to the goals each man wants to achieve.

4. We encourage open sharing by listening and encouraging others. We strictly avoid judgment and ridicule.

5. We celebrate each accomplishment—even if it is not perfect, such as reducing a habit to acting out once every few days instead of several times a day. We do not require perfection in order to celebrate progress.

6. Each member should be honest and open to being vulnerable with others. This is especially important between accountability partners.

7. We pledge ourselves to growth—every member should be open to growth and change.

8. Every member of the group is asked to pray for every other member every day.

9. Every member should feel as if the group is his own and thus take ownership of it. Attendance and fidelity are musts for success in building healthy relationships.

STEP 3: *Basic meeting structure.*

1. Start with prayer. It needn't be long, but we should invite the Holy Spirit to be present.

2. Next, share blessings and challenges. Each person is given an opportunity to talk about blessings and challenges he has faced in the past week. Anytime a challenge is offered, a blessing must also be offered to balance out the challenge. This is also a way to get those who are caught in despair to think about how God has blessed them and thus start to break the cycle of shame.

3. Time of teaching or encouragement. This time varies depending on the needs within the group. For instance, we have talked about prayer, strategies to stop, working on action plans, encouraging accountability, and even reading excerpts of books on the subject and then discussing them. More than anything, we never wag a finger at someone for messing up. He has enough shame already. Rather, we try to stay positive and upbeat while still challenging each other to choose well.

We go over how accountability went that week. Everybody is paired with an accountability partner. Each man is asked to call his partner at least two times a week to check in. Thus, they ought to talk a minimum of four times. The group works best when accountability partners take charge of helping each other out. If someone doesn't make his calls, I ask him to do something special for his accountability partner the next week. This could be extra prayers, fasting, or some other loving act for him. Accountability always works best when true friends learn to enjoy serving and being around one another.

Focusing on an emphasis for the following week is also important. Generally a theme arises in each man's struggles, so it helps to focus on one part of the struggle in particular. We always emphasize taking things one day at a time. This should always be the goal rather than a longer time frame, so that unreasonable expectations don't come up.

4. Closing prayer. We do different things for this prayer. Usually we pray for the intentions of the men and their families.

STEP 4: *Group guidelines.*

Every man is asked to sign a covenant about the basics of accountability and the legal obligations of the group leader (e.g., reporting of abuse of minors). When he signs, he agrees to participate according to the guidelines set out in the written agreement.

About the Author

MARCEL LEJEUNE is Assistant Director at St. Mary's Catholic Center, at Texas A&M University, the largest campus ministry in the country. He is a sought-after speaker and author of *Set Free to Love: Lives Changed by the Theology of the Body* (Servant Books). Marcel has contributed to three other books and written numerous articles. He is a regular guest on national radio programs and has appeared on EWTN TV. Marcel and his wife, Kristy, have five children. He blogs at www.AggieCatholicBlog.org and can also be found at www.MarcelLeJeune.com.

BOOKS & MEDIA

A mission of the Daughters of St. Paul

As apostles of Jesus Christ, evangelizing today's world:

We are CALLED to holiness
by God's living Word and Eucharist.

We COMMUNICATE the Gospel message
through our lives and through all
available forms of media.

We SERVE the Church
by responding to the hopes and needs
of all people with the Word of God,
in the spirit of St. Paul.

For more information visit our Web site: www.pauline.org.

BOOKS & MEDIA

The Daughters of St. Paul operate book and media centers at the following addresses. Visit, call, or write the one nearest you today, or find us at www.pauline.org.

CALIFORNIA
3908 Sepulveda Blvd, Culver City, CA 90230	310-397-8676
935 Brewster Avenue, Redwood City, CA 94063	650-369-4230
5945 Balboa Avenue, San Diego, CA 92111	858-565-9181

FLORIDA
145 S.W. 107th Avenue, Miami, FL 33174	305-559-6715

HAWAII
1143 Bishop Street, Honolulu, HI 96813	808-521-2731

ILLINOIS
172 North Michigan Avenue, Chicago, IL 60601	312-346-4228

LOUISIANA
4403 Veterans Memorial Blvd, Metairie, LA 70006	504-887-7631

MASSACHUSETTS
885 Providence Hwy, Dedham, MA 02026	781-326-5385

MISSOURI
9804 Watson Road, St. Louis, MO 63126	314-965-3512

NEW YORK
64 W. 38th Street, New York, NY 10018	212-754-1110

SOUTH CAROLINA
243 King Street, Charleston, SC 29401	843-577-0175

TEXAS

Currently no book center; for parish exhibits or outreach evangelization, contact: 210-569-0500, or SanAntonio@paulinemedia.com, or P.O. Box 761416, San Antonio, TX 78245

VIRGINIA
1025 King Street, Alexandria, VA 22314	703-549-3806

CANADA
3022 Dufferin Street, Toronto, ON M6B 3T5	416-781-9131